TWO FLAGS - ONE HEART

Main cover pictures by Jarman Photography, Jersey

Sheila as a London Hospital student nurse. 1947.

TWO FLAGS - ONE HEART

SHEILA LE SUEUR

STARLIGHT PUBLISHING

www.aacbooks.co.uk

Published in September 2000 by
STARLIGHT PUBLISHING
Unit 3b, Barette Commercial Centre
La Route du Mont Mado, St.John
Jersey, Channel Islands, JE3 4DS

Graphic design by Island Imaging, Jersey

Printed by Cromwell Press, Wiltshire

ISBN 095256598

Care more than others think necessary.

Trust more than others think wise.

Serve more than others think practical.

Anonymous

THIS BOOK IS DEDICATED TO
MY SISTER ANNE
AND
HER CHILDREN
SHEILA, PATRICIA, MICHELE, ALISON AND
MATTHEW

PUBLISHERS NOTE

The Americans and the British speak the same language but
sometimes it comes out differently.
Please remember that our author has spent considerable time
on both sides of the Atlantic so, depending on where you live,
words, phrases, spelling etc. may not be what you're
used to.

CONTENTS

CHANNEL ISLAND YEARS

EXPATRIATE YEARS

RETIREMENT YEARS

FOREWORD

Sometime in the early spring of 1994 my sister Anne persuaded me to try cable TV so that I could watch the C-SPAN network.

She assured me that was the best way to fill my political cravings. I resisted for months because I did not want to pay another bill. Once more I was trying to live on a budget. At the time it seemed to me that I should at least give it a try. I contacted Cox Cable and I began to watch C-SPAN. My decision was a significant one because what I have learned from C-SPAN has changed my life.

It began with the coverage of the 50th anniversary of the D-Day landings in 1994. Memories burst into my consciousness. I was back in Jersey longing, waiting, and believing that our liberation from Nazi occupation was days, perhaps hours away. That I was oblivious to the carnage just a few short miles away shames me now. I remember the fury that I felt when none of the correspondents in Normandy gave so much as a glance our way.

When Steve Scully interviewed the war veterans telling their stories, the deep feeling of gratitude and affection that I felt for them made me a C-SPAN viewer for all time. Memorial Day 1997 I watched the first tape of the C-SPAN Alexis de Tocqueville series. I connected. I knew from that moment that I was driven to wherever the road would lead me. The journey continues and it is the purpose for this book.

I am an active member of New Frontiers for Learning at Mesa Community College in Mesa, Arizona. We are a peer led group that facilitates classes for one another. I had my subject.

I discovered that Alexis De Tocqueville and I had much in common. We were born just 60 airlines miles apart: he in the village of Tocqueville in Normandy, I in Jersey. He was an aristocrat and I am from an ordinary family with a Norman name. It is an old Jersey name dating back to the 1300s. He was raised by the family priest, Abbe Le Sueur. I share the name but we are not related.

De Tocqueville sailed on a ship from Cherbourg for New York City in 1831. He intended to study the American penitentiary system, renowned at that time. He discovered Democracy! The journey by sail ship took 38 days. No refrigerators; in those days they had live provisions on board, including an Alderney cow from the most northerly of the Channel Islands. My great grandmother, Sophie Le Brun, was born that year, 1831. I was linked. The fact that Alexis was born in 1805, which was 122 years before me, made no difference. I had a plan. I needed the teaching materials offered through the education department at C-SPAN.

I called several times. The teaching plans were for teachers. I was a nurse. What I knew were patient care plans. I became desperate. I asked for help at the college and made one more call to C-SPAN and luckily Joanne Wheeler, Manager of Education and Marketing Services, answered the telephone. I made my case. She was reluctant to send me more than the poster. I pleaded for the teaching plans. I begged her for them. Two days later I had a special delivery package from Joanne with everything that I needed, wanted, hoped for. It was wonderful. The rest, as they say, is history.

Eighteen months later I was able to facilitate classes for our group of senior learners. We explored "What is a Democracy," culminating in a town hall meeting. We looked at voter apathy. The program was deemed a success. Joanne Wheeler has been my motivator. She is a role model for what a TV network should be all about. She exemplifies excellence in every respect. I have had the privilege of meeting Brian Lamb when I visited C-SPAN in Washington DC June of 1999.

My editor, Martin Sommerness, Professor of Journalism at Northern Arizona University in Flagstaff, Arizona, was one of the developers of the teaching materials for the Tocqueville series. Joanne quite properly was unable to give me a contact number for him but by using all the ingenuity that being an American affords me, I contacted him. This book was born because of his persuasion that I should record my life, enduring five long years of enemy occupation (1940-1945).

The telling of my story has become the joy of my life and in it I have faithfully recorded my <u>memories</u> of growing up during the Occupation years. I offer them as a tribute to all of the Channel Islanders who endured those difficult years. It is also the story of a proud daughter of Jersey who became an American.

Professor Sommerness and Joanne Wheeler will forever be special people in my life. They have shown me a new way and created within me a curiosity that is boundless. They have marked my life and I care deeply for both of them.

Sheila Le Sueur
Mesa, Arizona

Spring 2000

ACKNOWLEDGEMENTS

Believe in the impossible because one day it may happen to you. It happened to me. I was able to tell my story because a wonderful group of people believed I could. I owe them a debt of gratitude and thanks that come from the very depth of my heart.

Barbara Thelander, director of Community Services at Mesa Community College, first proposed the notion I should write a book about growing up in occupied Europe during WWII. I told her there were many books about the war, and besides, I found talking about those years exhausted me. I went on my way and completely forgot about it.

It was Professor Sommerness, Professor of Journalism at Northern Arizona University, and one of the developers of the teaching materials for the C-SPAN series on Alexis de Tocqueville, who convinced me of the possibility. Furthermore he told me he would be my editor. He was taking a chance that few would be willing to take. I shall always be grateful he pushed me toward this wonderful project. It has given me immense pleasure and has afforded me the opportunity to honestly evaluate my life. Besides, I could not have imagined having an editor. I find it impressive.

Special thanks (words seem so inadequate) to Dick and Patsy Royer, and to Ray and Joan Kettel, for the hours of proof-reading and suggestions, for their patience and love, and for putting up with the many phone calls.

I am also grateful for the tons of support at the college, which I have received from my peers in New Frontiers for Learning in Retirement.

Thanks to Millicent Salm, the first friend I met from the group, for her love and support.

Special thanks to Lyn Hochstadter who, from day one, believed in me. Lyn did yeoman's work in helping me prepare for the classes, "What Is A Democracy," which I facilitated for our group at the college. She even went as far as to create my very own web page. It was on the Internet for the entire World to see.

Thanks to my sister, Anne, for all of her input and for helping me, and for sharing her memories of those Occupation years.

Special love to my nieces and nephew, for believing their aunt can do anything.

A special thanks to my niece Tricia (the naughty twin), who reminds me that this year my age will match my house number. She has graced this manuscript with her touch and incredible computer skills. I love her for being in my life.

Remembering Joanne Wheeler at C-SPAN, who basically gave me the admission ticket to this adventure and the teaching materials for the Tocqueville program. Wondering if Alexis himself and his beloved priest Abbe Le Sueur are quietly approving from their spot above.

My advice to others is to create your own adventure. The path is filled with special people. I am blessed. I am surprised. I am grateful. Only in America!

CHAPTER ONE

Beginnings

The simple fact that I am sitting here in front of a computer, something I never wanted, goes to show anything can happen to anyone at anytime. As I start this project, I am filled with so many emotions, some of which surprise me. I am excited and curious, somewhat apprehensive yet confident; I am compelled to push on not knowing where it will lead me. I have a sense that I shall enjoy the journey more than anyone shall. I have the confidence because I am an American. I have the papers to prove it, but it is more than that. I have lived, worked and enjoyed all the rights and privileges to which that has entitled me. It is the people who are America and their generosity of spirit is irresistible. Sometimes, especially at first acquaintance, it was rather annoying. The total belief that anything is possible can be misunderstood. I have struggled to understand that part of the American personality and I have also discovered that the very fact that I sit here today attempting this incredible notion of writing a book, proves that I now possess those very same qualities.

There is another more urgent reason. I am a World War II survivor and I feel an enormous sense of responsibility to record those experiences as I lived them. One absolute is in all of our lives: we cannot choose our parents, ethnic origin, village, town or country. In that way we are all truly equal. From that time, our lives are as different as our fingerprints. In general we all remember our birthplace. I was born on the Channel Island of Jersey. The Island, the largest of the group, covers an area of 45 square miles. It is best known for the beautiful Jersey cows, rich cream, the Jersey Royal potato and the absolutely delicious tomatoes. They have the best taste in the world. Recent years have seen the growth of the finance industry. This has been good for the economy of the Island but has been in conflict with some of the old traditions. I have no first-hand knowledge of this. I have learned of it through friends and from what

I read in the Jersey Weekly Post. Tourism has always been a major component of the Island economy.

Also, dare I say it, the Island is known for having given its name to the State of New Jersey! The Islands are located in the Bay of St.Malo. During the D-day Normandy landings in WWII they were right in the eye of the storm.

The Islands have an ancient and fascinating history. In 1066 they were part of the Duchy of Normandy when William the Conqueror defeated Harold of England at the Battle of Hastings. They have long been, and to this day are, autonomous. We are proud to be Channel Islanders. In the historic sense England belongs to the Islands, which will surprise most of the English!

My parents were Sydney and Margaret Le Sueur and I arrived two years after their marriage. I was loved and wanted, but our initial acquaintance got off to a rocky start. I was due to make my grand entry in May 1927, but I had decided to come into the world backwards; breech presentation is the technical term. Our family doctor turned me in the right direction and I arrived June 1, a robust five pounds.

The day of my delivery happened to be a Wednesday and I was often teased that Wednesday's child is full of woe, and initially, I did nothing to ruin that image. The story is that I cried from morning and through most of the night. My father came home from work and paced the floor with this bundle of joy on a cushion. He soon found the moment he stopped, I cried. There was a simple reason for this behavior; I was starving! These inexperienced young people sought advice from everyone and my formula was changed almost every day. Finally, a new brand, "Truefood", coincided with the right advice and I never looked back. In fact, I went on to win first prize in a baby show when 12 months old. The prize was a beautifully engraved, solid silver tablespoon. There was another fact worth noting: Dr. Mortimer Evans, our physician, had just come to the Island from the London Hospital and I was the only baby in the

Sheila following christening June 17th 1927 with proud new parents and Nanny Ingram.

Sheila age 3. 1931. It was following my first cut at a hairdresser, Turner and Plumbley in Broad Street.

Mandalay School Photo. Sheila is on the left, third row up (with the striped tie showing).

contest that had been vaccinated for smallpox. I have three large scars on my arm to this day to show and thank for that.

The London Hospital, located in Whitechapel in the East End of London, was founded in 1740. It was the largest voluntary hospital in the UK until the National Health era began in 1947. Dr. Evans had a major influence on my life and during the Occupation he promised me that when we were liberated, he would recommend me to The London Hospital Nursing School. He kept his word and I am a London Hospital nursing graduate. The London Hospital was the home of the Elephant Man. As student nurses we were shown his skeleton in the Medical School Museum. The notorious Jack the Ripper who preyed on prostitutes during the Victorian era is said to have performed his grisly murders in the area. His trademark was that he disemboweled these unfortunate women and this gave him the name of Jack the Ripper. He was never found but there were rumors that he was the son of a noble family. According to legend, a physician who vowed never to reveal the secret while family members were living knew the identity of the dreadful Jack. I seem to remember reading in the paper that the physician died and took the secret with him. A family friend told me this story before I left for the London because she believed that I was heading for dangerous territory. She need not have worried. The students were safe in bed at night. I once forgot to sign in following a day off. I was awakened and scolded for my carelessness. We were safe in Whitechapel.

Back to my dietary problems. I was always reminded that Truefood was the most expensive formula on the market, which explains why my tastes are simple: I like the best! I was an only child for seven years until another daughter came along. Anne was given no option; she got cow's milk. I relate this in a light-hearted manner but in a few years, the Islands were to be occupied by the German forces for five long years and our survival and the threat of starvation is one of my reasons for this story.

My parents, as were others, were caught in a terrible situation. How could anyone have known that in a few short years the Third Reich would occupy the Island? Our lives were forever changed and survival became a daily routine. The manner in which they and the other islanders coped is part of a human experience that is a story worth remembering forever.

Probably my life can be looked upon as ordinary, but it is mine and it is what I know best. I know where my strengths lie and the mistakes that I have made. Regrets are useless because one can never go back to the situation as the same person. That is encouraging. I look back at my life before the war, during the war, in England, back to Jersey and most surprisingly of all in the United States.

Jersey in the '30s was a wonderful place to grow up. If there was a Great Depression, as a child I was not aware of it. I never heard that word until I came to the States. Jersey has a beauty that is unique and spectacular. Summers are warm and sunny as a rule because of its location in the Gulf Stream. We all know the frailty of weather forecasts and the weather can be changeable. Growing up, I remember the days as warm and sunny and our playground was the beach. The Jersey coastline and sandy beaches are the most beautiful in the world. It has been written that Jersey is the Gem of the Sea. I never get over the feeling of pride and affection that I feel for my birthplace.

We all wore school uniforms and yes; Panama hats (a hand-woven hat made with straw like strips of the leaves of a tropical plant.) The first warm day, which I interpreted as summer, I would start pestering my mother to let me wear my summer uniform. She was not always in agreement. It was a big deal to me and I am not sure why. The summer uniform dresses were made of a cream-colored shantung material. This material was named after a Chinese province. It was very soft and comfortable. The material was a silk or silky fabric with an uneven surface. As I write, this I wonder why it disappeared from the market. A needs-no-ironing material of some sort no doubt replaced it.

Winter uniform meant gym frocks, which were worn over a blouse, just like we do with a jumper today. It was pleated and

Family photo. Top row, left to right: Father, Sidney Le Sueur, Auntie Lil Garrard; Mother, Margaret Le Sueur. Bottom Row left to right; Anne Le Sueur (age 4), Sheila Le Sueur (age 11).

Sheila, one of the first days of school, 1932. Left to right: Edna Ingram, Sheila (age 5), Mother, Margaret Le Sueur. In the background you see the Ommaroo Hotel where the American prisoners were taken in 1945 when we were liberated, and where they had their reunion in 1995.

Mr. and Mrs. O'Flaherty in their garden with Pauline (O'Flaherty) Campbell, 1946.

tied around our waist with a girdle (a cloth belt). When it rained we wore those miserably uncomfortable Wellington boots. I was a pupil at Mandalay School and I am grateful for that. It gave me by far the best school memories that I still cherish today. That is a very valuable foundation for any child. Mandalay friends remain as a part of my life today.

I also went to dancing school but that too got off to a rocky start. I was a shy child and talkative but only within the safety of the family. To be shy is agony. I was enrolled at Miss Boielle's dancing school. The tiny red shoes were bought and I suppose the uniform was as well. Excitedly, we arrived for the first class. I refused to leave my mother's side and the more she tried, the more I resisted. To this day I can feel how desperately I wanted to join in but I could not, would not, do so. I think that I was about three or four years old.

Later, I was a pupil at Miss Rimington's school, but even though I loved ballet, I was not destined for stardom. The exercise was good (green ballet shoes this time). A few years ago on one of my visits to Jersey I went to meet a friend at the hairdresser. The hairdresser was in the same building and same room where I had taken the dancing classes. It was in an instant a flashback. I lost all sense that I was meeting my friend who sat under the hair dryer. Memories flooded my mind and I was back in the class. I could see the pianist and hear the familiar sound of Chopin. I closed my eyes and savored the memory of those days so long ago. It was a moment that was warm and wonderful. I got into trouble once for dropping crumbs from a currant bun in the cloakroom. The currant buns were delicious and a tasty snack after school.

Mandalay was a private school for boys and girls. It had a good scholastic reputation and the school colors were maroon and cream. Coats were navy blue and we wore berets. Boys, of course, wore caps and the usual things, but I cannot picture them now. Uniform was compulsory and although it must have been expensive, at least there were no arguments. Uniforms identified the school and were worn with pride. Mrs. Benton owned the school. She was the principal. I remember her as a gracious lady who was firm but kind.

Discipline the order of the day and part of our times. There was no physical form of punishment. Classes were small and if we were naughty or disobedient every one knew it. Embarrassment was a great deterrent. I must emphasize again that this was the right school for me. I have only positive memories. However, there was one exception: poetry class. We had to recite Wordsworth's poem "Daffodils" and once again I was stricken with paralyzing shyness. My best friend Pamela (we were glued together) had a similar attack of nerves. I refused and the miserable teacher put us both on a table together in front of the class and told us to recite the poem. I uttered not one word as I remember and the teacher must have given up. To this day I remember that poem. Now such an act might be considered child abuse and parents would be at the school in a second. In those days, the teacher had absolute control. I do not remember this individual, but she did nothing to endear me to poetry.

On a special occasion we were taken to the Opera House to see the motion picture Treasure Island. Peg Leg Pete terrified me and I walked out. I can still see my mother's look of surprise when I walked in the house. I don't recall asking for permission to leave the cinema but surely I must have done so. I was a polite child, even if I was a sissy! Christmas in the 1930's was fun with the school play and the parties. Parties were a must and invitations were brought to school like Valentines today. We wore party dresses and velvet cloaks and ballet shoes. The mothers served Jelly (Jell-O) and Blancmange (custard-like pudding set in a mold). We were always told to eat our bread and butter. This was a regular part of our teatime each day. Somehow Jell-O and bread in my mouth at one and the same time tasted horrible to me. The parties were fun; we played games and usually took a prize home. Our fathers came to take us home. My father had the use of a car so I grew up thinking that was normal. A car for every household was not a reality in the '30s. Christmas was eagerly anticipated. Mother spent hours preparing the Christmas puddings and the Christmas cake. In those days, the fruit took hours to clean and prepare. Christmas Day was the only time we had turkey and I still only like the white meat. The incentive to eat the Christmas pudding was to find the silver charms and the silver coins (sixpences) that were cooked inside the pudding. Now, I need no such incentive because they are delicious. We had to be in the drawing room at 3 o'clock to listen to the King's Christmas message. The drawing room is the front room or parlor. We always used ours; it was never saved for guests only. That's when the Christmas cake was served and the attraction there was the almond paste and icing. A Christmas cake is a tradition, which we keep to this day. It has no resemblance to the American version. A Christmas cake is a fruitcake covered with almond paste and icing. They are beautifully decorated. My mother once made one of a lady in a crinoline gown. The top and head of the body was made of porcelain. We continue to make this part of our holiday tradition. Luckily Anne makes one every year from our mother's recipe.

Soon I was at the age 12 and it was time to advance to another school. My best friend Pam and I took the entrance exam for a public school (a state school) and we both were successful. The month before I had spent a holiday with a family friend of my parents in Guernsey. This was a major undertaking for me. I took the mail boat by myself and actually left home! My parents must have been astonished and probably crossed their fingers that this time it would work. Guernsey was too far for the bedtime call " I want to come home now."

This was a very happy time; Auntie Lill was very kind to me. Years later I tried to find her. Her niece, Mary, who I remembered as a young college student, told me that she survived the German Occupation but died soon after from leukemia. During that holiday I can recall frequent trips to the sweet (candy) shop where I bought many packets of Rollo candy. Calories and cholesterol were a long way from the vocabulary in the '30s. I also remember the popular song on the wireless was *Red Sails in the Sunset*. It was played repeatedly. I never liked it and I shall always associate it with the start of WWII.

I had to return home to the new school and the war began September 3, 1939. I remember being in the dining room as the 11 a.m. announcement came on the wireless. My parents told us that this was very serious. They remembered WW1. That war did not come to Jersey, but my father served, as did others. Channel Islanders volunteered; they were not enlisted. The UK is responsible for our protection and our men volunteer to "do their bit," incredible as that may seem today. We were extremely patriotic and that stood us in good stead during the ordeal that was to follow.

The time went by, everyone was confident that the Maginot Line would hold. The battleship Graf Spee was sunk off the coast of South America. We were not surprised; we expected victory. Spring arrived and the news on the wireless was not as expected. No one could have imagined what was to follow. Jersey did not seem to be threatened and life went on happily as ever. The wily Fuhrer had other plans for us. The Channel Islands were British territory and he could hardly wait to claim us. My parents said that if the Germans came it would only be an "old officer" who would be stationed at Government House. This is the residence of the King or Queen's representative in the Island. These officials are usually retired officers from the armed services and have no judicial power over Island laws or government. That supposition was wrong and more than wrong. The Home Office in London, which was responsible for the Islands, saw no need to provide protection and was deaf to requests for guidance from the Islands. By June 1940, the Islanders began to experience the horrors before them: evacuation, air raids and bombs. The Islanders were bracing themselves for enemy Occupation. Such are the fortunes of war. Our lives were to change forever.

CHAPTER TWO

Evacuation, Sounds of War and Bombs

Evacuation. According to *Webster's New World Dictionary* the definition of evacuation is to make empty, to discharge, to withdraw. My definition: fear, panic, uncertainty, and June 1940. Our island home, Jersey, was about to be occupied by orders from the Fuhrer himself: Adolph Hitler.

The shock of war slowly subsided and life went on as usual after September 3, 1939. The new school was a big adjustment, larger classes, further away from home. It was no longer possible to go home for dinner (we ate our main meal at noontime) in those days. Gone were the sheltered days at Mandalay School. The new school was in an old building with dark corridors and the playground was bare blacktop. It was all rather depressing as I look back at it now. My friend and I made for the back row in the classroom, which was exactly the last place we should have been seated. A year or so later I had my first eye exam and needed glasses. I must have missed a lot of good information on the blackboard.

News from the outside world came from two sources. The BBC news on the wireless and the English newspapers. At mealtime my parents would discuss the situation as the news became more and more unsettling. I seem to remember that it sounded scary but not as scary as it should have been. When it became obvious that France would fall, consternation increased. As a 13 year old, I do not believe that any of us really imagined that the Island would be occupied. What did being occupied mean? Clearly no one really knew. Life at my level remained unaltered. When France was lost and British troops passed through Jersey to England, reality set in.

On June 19th, 1940, Jersey was declared a demilitarised zone. The Lieutenant Governor, the British troops and the Jersey Militia left the Island and the possibility of *Evacuation* began in earnest. Potatoes and tomatoes continued to be loaded on merchant ships to England but now civilians were given the opportunity to leave. The panic began. My mother refused to leave without my father. There was talk of sending my sister and I to my mother's family in America. Some friends had already gone. Farmer friends could not leave their cattle so the decision for them was more easily settled.

A ship from the Shell Petrol Company was due to arrive and my father thought that we could leave on that. They joined hundreds of others in a queue at the Town Hall where the necessary papers were issued. We were left in the car parked by the Parade Gardens. They could not leave their place in the queue. We were there for hours. Finally, friends who were farmers and who could not leave their livestock took us home. Our parents eventually arrived home in the early hours of the morning. These were incredible days. My mother for once was completely disorganized. She only packed the family silver. Once she was heard to remark that maybe she should turn the gas on and end it all and all of us. No one took her seriously. My father would come back and forth with news updates. Everything was uncertain. To evacuate, to leave their home with two children and face the uncertainty of life in England was difficult to comprehend. Where would they go and where would my father work? What a horrifying experience for them, and the other Islanders who were facing the same fate. Security was slipping away with every minute.

Rumors were rife and the major topic was who had left and who was staying. Some fled leaving toast in the toaster and thousands of pets were destroyed at the Animal Shelter. This beautiful and peaceful island was in an uproar. The population in Jersey was 50,000 in 1939, and when the Island was occupied 40,000 residents had decided to remain and face whatever was before them. Possibly greater numbers would have gone but the transportation ships available were at a minimum. I do not remember if we went to school during this time. I know that many of the teachers who were English left and that was certainly understandable.

We had a solid and sensible Island leader in Alexander Coutanche. He was the Bailiff and head of judicial and civil affairs of the Island. I need to remind the reader that the Channel Islands, although no longer part of Normandy, had retained many of the Norman customs and the Norman laws. Mr. Coutanche was an Advocate of the Royal Court. After the war he became Lord Coutanche. Those of us who survived the next five years did so because of his courage and tenacity in dealing with the occupying forces. Baron von Aufsess in his account *"Occupation Diary"* described our Bailiff as "That wily old lawyer." One might say now, "It takes one to know one." Mr. Coutanche calmed the Islanders when he stated that he and his wife planned to stay. My parents had great confidence in his leadership. He proved himself to be a remarkable individual. He was our anchor and outmanoeuvred the occupying forces time and time again. The people of Jersey were his priority and their most urgent need for the next five years was the food supply.

Thoughts of going to England were pretty exciting. We continued to play on the beach; planes flying overhead did not seem to bother us. For some inexplicable reason, on June 28th, we (my friend and both of our sisters and a small neighbor girl) decided to go to visit my Aunt Rita and play on the beach in front of her house. The house was on the beachfront. The beach stretched for two or three miles. It was separated from the road by a handsome granite wall. There were steps down to the beach. This was the other side of the Island from our home and very unusual for us to do this. The tide was out that afternoon. It alternates each week morning and afternoon. I always liked high tide because we could go swimming and it was fun with the waves rolling in. Jersey tides are unique and hazardous and the waters around the Islands have been described as some of the most dangerous in the world. The sea can creep up around the rocks trapping the unwitting tourist. There is good fishing at low tide and this is best left to the locals.

Back to June 28th. I remember it well. It was a day with a hazy cloudy sky. There were planes flying overhead all afternoon. They were German reconnaissance planes. Today, it seems incredible that we did not realize this. My mother knew where we were; no one was prepared and apparently not alarmed. There was no sense that a dangerous enemy was closing in on our Island. The seagulls had been flying all around us and seemed to be unusually annoying that day. I have often wondered if they were warning us. Or maybe they were just hoping for food scraps.

When it was time to go home we went up to my aunt's house. We were just saying good-bye when we all heard a loud bang. Auntie Rita reassured us that it probably was a load of potatoes falling off a lorry at the Weighbridge. Auntie Rita was my father's older sister. She was rather an innocent person, a loving aunt. I thought the world of her. The Weighbridge was where the farmers took their lorries loaded with produce (potatoes and tomatoes) to be weighed before being loaded on to the ships in the harbor for transport to England. It was a building with a built-in scale where the farmers would drive their lorries through it and moved forward on to the docks. During the season the lorries were lined up for quite a long wait. This was the scene in Guernsey when the Germans bombed the Islands. Dozens of farmers took shelter under their vehicles and were incinerated. The Germans assumed that the trucks were loaded with munitions.

Off we went to catch the bus and were on our way. As I recall, we were the only passengers. This was unusual. It turned into the ride of our young lives. We had just turned into the road opposite the General Hospital. There was a succession of very loud noises, which we were too young to identify. No one knew much about war and all of its horrors. The bus driver acted promptly. He stopped the bus and told the five of us to get out and run to the trenches in the gardens. Once more we were in the Parade Gardens, which were opposite the hospital. The trenches were only recently dug in order to provide some kind of protection. We did as we were told.

Gillian was a tiny girl and remembers it very clearly. Her account is printed on page 28. I recall looking up to the sky and I can still see the plane overhead. I know exactly where it was in the sky. I shall never forget it. We were in an air raid. The explosions of the bombs dropping were the noises that we heard.

There was gunfire all around us. It was all so fast and so unreal. I cannot recall fear; I think that I remember the driver telling us to get out of the bus.

He was calm just as though this was part of his bus route. He was one cool dude as one might say over here in the States. I covered Gillian with my body. Pam did the same for her sister, also named Anne. The bus driver covered my sister Anne. I was babysitting Gillian. It is interesting that I protected her and not my sister. I felt responsible because I was taking care of her that afternoon. It was all unplanned. We reacted to the situation and the bus driver took charge of all of us.

May 1995 was the golden anniversary of our Liberation. Some months prior, those wonderful celebration survivors were invited to write in to the Jersey Evening Post with stories of their experience during the Occupation. Gillian, after much persuasion, agreed to write her memories of the bombing. As I remember, she was very quiet and held on to my hand without a whimper. She was a very tiny little girl. Eventually the bombing stopped and I suppose the planes returned to France. The Islands had no means of resisting the assault.

The bus driver loaded us back on to the bus and followed the usual route, which took us to the bus stop near our home. I was 13 years old and I cannot imagine now why I was not absolutely terrified. I did not cry until I saw my anxious father waiting for us at the bus stop. The five of us had followed the bus driver's leadership with implicit faith. Perhaps we were too busy to cry. We probably had no real idea of what was happening.

Gillian remains a special friend until this day. War and bombs were as foreign to us as the Germans. Eleven people died that day and many others were injured. We were lucky to have escaped our ordeal unharmed.

The JMT bus driver (Jersey Motor Transport) drove the bus undeterred until we were all safely home. An incredible individual devoted to duty, with extraordinary courage. I hope that his bravery was recognized, but I fear not. The Island was in turmoil and lives were being disrupted. The only certainty was the uncertainty of what was before us.

There were further air raid warnings and a lot of air activity. The Germans were testing, and when it was clear that there was no resistance they made plans to occupy the Islands. The civil authorities received the ultimatum and the population was ordered to display white flags as a sign of surrender. If this was done the "life, property, and *liberty* of all peaceful citizens" was guaranteed. Prisoners of war have no *liberty*.

The next day the swastika was flying from all major buildings. The Occupation officially began July 1, 1940. The liberty we had been promised ceased to exist. Five long years were ahead of us. Perhaps it is better that we never know the future. The telephone cable to England was severed and we were cut off from all that was familiar to us. The Jersey people demonstrated their natural independence and creativity during the next five miserable years. It was never easy, but we never ever doubted victory.

I have found myself reluctant to begin this part of my story, feeling the need to take a deep breath. It is like climbing a mountain; it is so hard to describe how I feel. Recently an enormous amount of attention has been given to World War II: movies and books on the bestseller lists. Veterans of that era once so silent about their experiences are beginning to tell their tales. Many wonder how they could have remained silent for so long. In a sense, I understand their silence. Those of us who lived it each experienced it in our own way. Our memories are unique and for the Islanders they are probably as different as our personalities. We do share a common bond; we understand freedom lost.

Gillian Hart

■ *Gill Hart, now Mrs Willis, was a small girl when the Occupation began, but her first experience of it was never to be forgotten.*

'MY Occupation story is a tribute to an unknown JMT bus driver who really was an unsung hero.

'It all happened when the Island was bombed the day before the Occupation, shortly before my fourth birthday.

'We were a group of five children living near the recreation grounds at St Clement. Our names were Sheila and Anne Le Sueur, aged 12 and five; Pamela Millard, who was 12, her sister Anne, and me — Gillian Hart, the youngest and by far the smallest. My mother was ill with yet another migraine, so Sheila was looking after me.

'We usually played together on the beach at Grève d'Azette, but for some unknown reason we had travelled to St Aubin's Bay where we went on the sands below First Tower.

'It was low tide, and ominously — which we did not appreciate — we were entirely alone, with many planes flying around. Suddenly there was an enormous bang which greatly frightened us — so we quickly made our way to the nearby home of Rita Le Sueur.

'Auntie Rita was not too concerned, suggesting that the noise was just potatoes being dropped at the Weighbridge. However, she thought that it would be wiser if we caught the next bus back into town.

'The planes were still flying around when we children climbed on to the bus — which was promptly buzzed by a German plane. The scene was chaotic, and, as we were the only passengers and absolutely terrified, the concerned driver drove straight to the air-raid shelters in the Parade. While the air raid continued, Sheila shielded me with her body in the open trench; Pam lay on top of her younger sister while the driver protected Anne Le Sueur.

'After a while, the driver decided that we should make a run for it. Instead of just dropping us off at the Weighbridge bus station, he continued towards our homes, still pursued by the plane.

'Arriving at the Ryburn Road entrance at Green Road, we found that a very worried Syd Le Sueur was anxiously searching for us.

'I can remember screaming as we ran towards our homes in nearby Ryburn Avenue. The brave driver then carried on towards Millard's Corner, where he dropped off the Millard sisters at their home. The whole incident affected me deeply and gave me nightmares for many years afterwards.

Excerpt from '60 Years On' feature, Jersey Evening Post, 28th June 2000.

Bombing of St. Helier Harbour, 28th June 1940.

A number of small boats were damaged in the bombing.

After the war the opportunities of freedom were dazzling. I pushed the memories of those five long years out of consciousness confident that nothing like that could ever happen to anyone again. When I am with someone who shared those years, remembering is almost comforting. They are almost impossible to describe. Survival is an indelible experience.

Also, I live in the United States and mention of those times invokes great sympathy and I feel somewhat guilty because I was never in a camp, nor did I fight in battle. Friends tell me that they had ration cards and gasoline was scarce. How do I explain there was nothing left in the shops? The barter system was born and it became a cottage industry. It was literally a lifesaver. I stress the fact that the shelves in the shops were empty! The human spirit is a great survivor and it is so often underestimated. The Jersey people put creativity to the test.

In the next chapter I shall do my best to re-ignite those memories as I lived them. I would never want to repeat any of them, but in a subtle way I am grateful for them. I am truly proud to belong to the World War II generation.

As I write this in 1999 and having just read the Memoirs of Lord Coutanche, I am more proud than ever to have grown up in Jersey during his tenure in office. Alexander Coutanche was the quintessential Jerseyman. He will always be a hero to me.

CHAPTER THREE

The Occupation Years
1940 - 1945

As I start to write about this time in my life, the memories seem to be both real and unreal. There are many scholarly works that record the history of those years. These are my memories of how I lived those years, written almost sixty years later. I am surprised that these feelings and memories surface so quickly. The years melt away and we are back in Jersey as a family. The decision not to evacuate was a relief and in a sense life settled down. The white flags were hung as ordered and humor imposed itself once more. A friend hung a baby's nappy (diaper) from her window and we all thought that this was quite amusing.

The Island authorities informed the Germans of our intent to surrender peacefully and, sure enough, by late afternoon about 100 German troops and officials arrived at the airport. The Bailiff, the Government Secretary and the Attorney General met them. The Bailiff had instructed the Islanders that resistance would be useless. A calm approach was the order of the day. On an island of 45 square miles there was no easy hiding place; few people possessed guns: many of the male population of military age had left the Island to volunteer for the British armed forces.

The Union Jack was replaced by the Swastika and communications with England and the rest of the world, including the other Channel Islands, ceased. Certainly in our family and circle of friends the expectation was that this was a temporary arrangement. Everyone was confident that victory would be achieved within months. The German expectations were the same. Everyone was wrong.

As I look around the world today it seems incomprehensible that anyone could be so naive. We had believed Neville Chamberlain when he proclaimed "Peace in our time." No one realized how unprepared Britain was from a military point of view. Winston Churchill began to be our hero and without him it is difficult to even think of where we would be now. I can see myself in a classroom at Mandalay School and I remember feeling such a sense of relief in 1938 when we were promised peace.

The feelings of an 11 year old are difficult to explain at this point in my life. I do remember how frightening it was seeing the Movietone News as the pictures of the fighting in China appeared on the screen. My movie experience was strictly limited to Shirley Temple and I longed to have curls like Shirley but that never happened!

The news that had dominated the attention in the '30s was the abdication of Edward, uncrowned King of England. I remember all the talk about Wallis Simpson and there was plenty of it, but it seemed to be in a more respectable frame of reference than we would expect today.

World War 1 had produced inconveniences in Jersey but these were minimal when compared to WWII. Sugar and petrol were rationed. Young Jerseymen who had volunteered for the armed forces were being killed or gassed on the Western front. The Jersey Militia left the Island for the same reason, to aid in the fight. There was anxiety and concern but there were no wireless sets in those days, so communication was by letter and newspaper. I clearly remember getting our first wireless set. That was in the early 1930s. Mother often talked of the day the war ended in 1918 and how she ran into the town to celebrate wearing her apron! My father had volunteered for the Royal Naval Air Service and done his "bit" as it was referred to at that time. This was a new branch of the armed forces and made necessary with the advent of airplanes.

My father had a mechanical mind and there was nothing that he could not do with an engine. Sadly, he died in 1952 and never knew that one day he would have a granddaughter, Sheila, who is an engineer.

The last time Jersey was invaded it was by the French in 1781 and they were soundly defeated. In 1940, no one knew what to expect, but my parents either believed that this would be a benign occupation or perhaps they wanted to reassure my sister Anne and me. That was the impression that I recall today. Certainly no one could have conceived of a Hitler or the Holocaust.

So the Occupation started and for that first afternoon there was no sign of the enemy. The family went to bed that night and I do not remember feeling any sense of fear. I suspect that my parents were full of anxieties. My father went to work the next morning as usual. Apparently there was no school, because the next morning I was riding my bike when a lorry (truck) swept past me and it was full of German soldiers. I remember the shock and I went as fast as I could peddle to my father who worked at the Cleveland Garages.

Mother got into action. She began many trips into the town to stock up on food supplies. The German forces seized the same opportunity. They shopped until they dropped, so to speak, happy to find luxuries long denied them. Some of them thought that they were already in England. Many businesses in the Island had coats of arms on their walls "By appointment to the King." This impressed them and no doubt helped their superiors to urge them on to final victory.

My sister and I discovered a secret supply of chocolates, which our mother had hidden in her bedroom wardrobe. We looked at them longingly, but we never helped ourselves. Mother was a strict disciplinarian about things like that. I can remember the wrapper but not the name of these chocolates. Eventually we ate all of them. There were no refills; this was *Occupation.*

A ration, a new word in our vocabulary, was part of daily life. Butter, sugar, and cooking fat (4oz) meat (3/4lb) per person per week. At the end of the ordeal this would have been regarded as generous, a banquet, really. The Germans loaded barges with Jersey tomatoes and potatoes (Jersey Royals) and transported them to France in just two months together with the prize cattle. Jersey cows are the most beautiful in the world and I did not know that any other breed existed until I went to England in 1945. What I saw there did nothing to change my mind. As regards Jersey tomatoes and potatoes, they are the best tasting in the world. Pride may be involved here but once tasted, the flavor is never forgotten. Many years later I brought a basket of tomatoes back to the States. They had ripened to perfection and the customs officer took them away from me. I was so angry. He gave me one withering look when I suggested that he had taken them to eat them. I often wondered what he did with them. They were perfect and I was looking forward to enjoying them! The law is the law!

Hitler delighted in what he called his "Island Fortresses" and the troops reportedly believed they now occupied British soil. The Channel Islands were not England. The Germans believed their own propaganda that the war would be over in three weeks. Many years would pass and unbelievable horrors were before them not, the least being the Russian front.

The Evening Post was ordered to publish a daily edition for distribution to the troops titled "Deutsche Inselzeitung" and touted by the Editor, a Dr. Kindt, as the first German newspaper issued in the British Empire. Perhaps he and Hitler were impressed, but I doubt that the locals shared their sentiments.

Memories of the next few months are blurred to me, school no doubt resumed and we learned to live with a lot of restrictions, rules, and warnings. For example, cameras were confiscated. Not all of the Jersey people complied and some were arrested for espionage when photos of fortifications were found in their possession. These individuals were taken to France and imprisoned in the camps. Several of them died in captivity.

We were required to carry identity cards. The photos were probably the only ones taken of us for the entire Occupation. The quality was poor as I remember. I know that I lost mine too often and presumably my parents got it replaced. My father thought I was never going to make it through life. He would send me into the kitchen for a fork and I would come back with a cup. He was often exasperated, but it seemed to have no effect on either my memory or me. I take great comfort from this personality trait now; it is reassuring to know that any forgetfulness cannot be attributed to advancing age. Truth is my thoughts move faster than my memory can keep up with them.

We had to learn to ride our bikes on the "wrong" side of the road as in Germany and the United States and France. Come to think of it, perhaps England is different from the rest of the world in that respect. Civilian cars were gone and we walked a lot. Sterling, as currency was gone. The Occupation Reichmarks became the legal tender of the day. Blackout curtains were compulsory. My father made frames for black paper that had to be in place at nightfall each evening. This was my rotten job for five long years. I clearly remember the day and how it felt when liberation freed me from this chore. It is strange to look back now at such a simple task, but at the time it felt like such a burden. Eventually we had no electricity or any form of light, but still the blinds went up every night.

All of these changes followed one on top of the other and it is nothing short of remarkable how life can change and how deep the ability to adapt is inherent in the human being.

Our lives formed a pattern of co-existence; we ignored the enemy as much as we could. My parents were totally absorbed in our survival. I realize that an even greater closeness among friends was a good result of this Occupation. Friends helped one another and the barter system became a lifesaver. We kept chickens and one noisy, pushy rooster. He fancied himself and would strut around the garden. We had eggs that were a bona fide currency on the barter system.

Food supplies became difficult. Anne and I collected seaweed (caragreen moss) from the sea. The Jersey name for seaweed is *vraic* and it was used as a fertilizer. It was a common sight to see farmers with their horse and wagons on the beach collecting it. The tide comes in and the seaweed is pushed forward with each wave. I used to feel squeamish running through it wondering about what I might step on when I went in for a swim. Our mother made some kind of ersatz Jell-O substance from this, a new slant on creative cooking. The seawater was boiled to provide salt. It takes a lot of it for an amount as small as a tablespoon. There was a military zone surrounding the beaches, so it had to be obtained during specific hours. I distinctly recall a mission almost accomplished one afternoon. We were climbing over the sea wall and someone dropped one of the bottles. It broke into a million pieces and the salt water was gone. It was just before curfew time so the opportunity was gone for one more day.

Some people kept rabbits and, yes, they multiply, war or no war! I used to go with my friend "rabbiting." We walked all over to collect food for these little creatures, every evening at least during the summer months we searched for greens. We lived close to a golf course and we became excellent "groundskeepers." My father would not have anything to do with rabbits, primarily I believe because of their ability to produce little bunnies at such an alarming rate. Maybe he did not think of separating the sexes. However, we had chickens and Anne reminded me that Dad made some kind of an incubator and the chicks were hatched that way. As we talked I remembered that some of these little chicks needed some help with the process so we had a chicken nursery of sorts in the house. They were kept warm thanks to the Aga cooker (stove) and finally joined their brothers and sisters in the garden. When we moved into the house in 1935, Dad built a pit for compost and the like. It is still there today. For months after the war we found eggs in the pit.

There were no luxuries. Most who owned a garden grew their vegetables and once again creative dishes were produced. At that time I believe we still had fuel for our Aga cooker. This kept the house warm in the winter and was the source for the hot water.

Carrots were burned for tea. Acorns were ground for coffee. Jam was a thing of the past. The bread was a dark brown heavy substance, which grew moldy overnight if there was any left over, which was not often. The changes in our diet wreaked havoc with the gastrointestinal tract and a new diagnostic term was coined, "The Local Complaint." I went to school one day with a friend who had only eaten boiled carrots for a week and she had all she could do to push her bike up the hill.

One day I came home for dinner from school and all that we had to eat was a can of Mulligatawny soup and a can of pears. I do not remember feeling ill, but when I got back to school I started vomiting. I had developed Infectious Hepatitis. Dr. Evans was called and he made the diagnosis. My complexion turned a deep orange and I had all the accompanying symptoms of the illness. I became quite confused; there were no medications and certainly no intravenous fluids at that time. There was a small amount of white flour in the Island for the diabetics and he ordered some for me. My mother did what she could to feed me but I still remember how ill I felt. Anyone who has had hepatitis will know exactly how it felt. One is completely drained of energy for a long time.

About that time the meat supply must have been critical. We had a two-story home; the bedrooms and the bathroom were upstairs. I remember my parents hanging a pig from the banisters to drain the blood out of it. Presumably they had obtained it from a farmer who slaughtered it unknown to the Germans. This porker ended up in a barrel in my bedroom. It was soaking in brine. We had a neighbor, a butcher, whom I presume cut it in pieces. I remember being confused seeing this barrel at the foot of my bed but remember nothing else about the first days of the illness. The meat was pure brine and starvation would have been more palatable. I was ill for months and looked like a skeleton. Dear Dr. Evans attended me faithfully and slowly I recovered. To this day I have not been able to eat a pear and whatever the soup was I would know it in a minute if it were served to me. Dr. Evans arranged for me to have a dog named "Dusty". He was a Dandie Dinmont and he had a penchant for chasing cats.

I remember one day I let go of the leash and he took off after a cat right into a butcher shop. I arrived breathless to the rescue to find the butcher up on the counter. Dusty had to be put down a few years later. I realize now that he must have developed nephritis. It was a terrible loss. I loved him and he loved me. Dusty, according to Webster's, was a terrier, a small, active dog with drooping ears, short legs and a rough coat, usually gray or tan, of a breed originated in Scotland. Dusty was gray and he had a brother named Rusty. He was given to me to encourage me to get out after the months of recovering from Hepatitis. Apparently he had a history of being tough on cats! He had the biggest brown eyes and faithful disposition.

I cannot say that once well I was always eager to take him for his walk so the lot fell to my mother. I do remember that the night before he died, he struggled up the stairs to be with me. I was doing my homework in my bedroom. As I write this there are tears in my eyes and I am reminded how much all of my pets have filled spaces in my life. Time does not dim the pleasure of their company or the affection so freely given.

Before the end of the Occupation and after Dusty we were given a cat named Paddy. He was a real sweetheart and gray in color similar to Dusty. Feeding these animals during the Occupation was never easy. A neighbor who worked at the slaughterhouse supplied us with udders from the cows for Dusty, and Paddy ate boiled limpets. We only had to touch the lid of the saucepan and Paddy would come running. He heard that sound almost faster than any of us. Limpets are small shellfish that are harvested from the rocks at low tide. Mother bought these at the fish market in town. She would boil them and the smell was horrendous. I do not remember much about the "udders" and I can hardly bear to think about it now. After the war, Paddy's diet much improved. He dined on boiled cod. He was so patient even as far as allowing my sister Anne to dress him in doll's clothes. He would sleep for hours in her doll's pram and made for a lot of amusements running around dressed like a baby.

There were some lighter moments. Occasionally, my parents would have parties and that meant guests staying until morning because of the curfew. There was a curfew for all of the five years -

I do not remember the exact hours. Certainly it was from dark until dawn. One night, when one of these parties was in progress, two German soldiers rang the doorbell. They said they were lonely for their families and that they were Polish conscripts forced into the German army. I can hear my mother now telling my father to get them out of the house. We had no desire to collaborate with the enemy. We shall never know if their story was true.

From all that I have read, the average German soldier was well behaved. It would seem that their greatest problem was being separated from their families. After the Normandy landings, hunger was a major problem for the soldiers. The civilian population felt no obligation to share with them. It became the survival of the fittest. During the Occupation many of the soldiers enjoyed the Channel Islands and some of them considered this posting as a holiday. I cannot help thinking that many of them preferred hunger to fighting in Normandy in 1944. It is impossible to hate individuals whom one never met and now I only see a uniform and hear boots on the pavement. The enemy is an intruder without face, personality or family. I also feel revulsion and a degree of resentment. Is this pathological? Absolutely not, but I do understand the feelings of any people whose territory is invaded by the enemy. Freedom is so precious and even the longest life lived is too short to be wasted. Hitler invested huge resources and manpower in his obsession with the Channel Islands much to the frustration of his generals, many of whom feared for their lives if they resisted his flawed military judgment. I find it fascinating that these individuals were powerless to stamp out the cancer in their society.

One last word. I believe the Germans in Jersey had an easy war. They were not in Normandy on D-Day. Perhaps some of them never saw any action. Boredom does not bleed. Many of the British and American veterans are my friends and it is almost impossible to express the gratitude to them for our lives and liberation. We could see and hear the gunfire in Normandy but never could have imagined the horror of the battles. That goes for both sides, Allied and German troops.

As I try to remember the Occupation, I am finding the memory doesn't come in chronological order; I trust that the reader will allow me to reminisce as the thoughts come to mind.

My parents had a lot of friends who came to visit us and use our Aga cooker that also heated the hot water. Both were much appreciated. There was the "bath group" who came for a weekly bath. Presumably they had some kind of brush because there was no soap. I remember that I did not like one individual in particular using our bathtub. I never said anything to my parents, now I wonder if these people cleaned the tub after using it. Knowing my mother she would have cleaned it anyway. I hope so! She was a meticulous housekeeper, but when she got married she did not know how to cook. After eating chips (French fries) for days on end my father asked her "You do know how to cook ?" "Absolutely," she assured him!

She must have been a fast learner for she certainly was a good cook ever since I can remember. My father believed in keeping a good table. I remember him saying that the English did not do this, but I do not know the basis for his belief. We always had good plain food and plenty of it. My mother was a wonderful pastry cook. She excelled in mince pies and maid of honors. Maid of honors are small tartlets filled with a jam and almond filling. They are delicious and loaded with calories just like all the good stuff usually is! She made tasty sausage rolls, another of my favorites.

Tea time was at 4 p.m. Bread and butter with jam, dainty sandwiches and cakes or pastries were usually served. It was not uncommon for Dad to arrive home with fresh fish that he bought from the fishermen as they came into harbor. This would be served for high tea about 6:30 or 7 p.m. That was normal meal patterns for us. So we basically ate four meals a day; breakfast, dinner, tea, and high tea and whatever we wanted before bed. That does not count fruit and candy (sweets) during the day. My Mother had long since perfected her culinary skills and they were put to the test during the hungry years. Fair to say that she excelled in this art. Something her eldest daughter never aspired to achieve. If we had an especially good meal during the Occupation, we never discussed it outside of the home. This would be food that was not obtained on the ration. The reason for the secrecy was fear of an informer.

In recent times much has been written about the Occupation. It has almost become a cottage industry of sorts, particularly for those who subscribe to the "gotcha" phenomena. These stories have been written by people born years, even decades, after the war. They describe and exaggerate, suggesting collaboration with the Germans and in doing so distort the truth. The truth is German soldiers fathered some children but the majority of the Jersey people were intensely patriotic and steadfast in their belief in victory. The children born of these liaisons were innocent victims of the war in a unique way. I have read that some had to deal with discrimination after the war. The locals knew those who collaborated with the Germans. They paid the price after the war. It is difficult to hide in a small island. My parents and their generation would think that the accusations were unbelievable. I say to these ill–informed authors, only we who lived through those years know the truth. They dishonor memory of my parents and their contemporaries. Shame on all who would dare to do so.

I have given a great deal of thought about the memories of the Occupation years. My mind has been trying to separate the years, but they remain a solid block in my mind. I cannot distinguish one from the other. I have no memory of birthdays or holidays, how we spent them or what we had to eat. What we had to eat would have been of special significance rather than gifts or the usual activities associated with such celebrations. The Occupation started one month after my 13th birthday and ended three weeks before my 18th birthday. These are normally very important years in the life of a young girl. I think my overall reaction now is that those years were best characterized as monotony. Difficult to imagine young people today tolerating such an existence. Certainly it must have been much more difficult for those who were 18 when it all started. No chances for higher education, career choice and so on. It is true that one never has to look far to find someone worse off than oneself.

I mentioned the pig hanging from the banisters. Such a waste of good Jersey pork which is absolutely delicious. No doubt rich in cholesterol and perfectly capable of clogging the coronary arteries in an instant. That was one hazard we did not face in our fat-starved dietary regime.

Anne reminded me that at one time we had the carcasses of not one but two cows in the house. A neighbor was a butcher and I do remember that the cows were cut up in the garage. We then had some fat from the suet. Jerseys are milk cows and really not suitable for meat because of the high fat content in their muscle. They provided us and the neighbors with some great meals. We needed the fat. Of note is that there were no freezers and of course no electricity in the latter years of the Occupation, and what we did have was rationed. I do not know who sold the cows to my father but they no doubt were slaughtered secretly because the Germans kept close tabs on the herds. We do know that our Father sold the meat to the neighbors at cost to him and it was not intended for nor did it make any profit.

I remember one dark early morning that the "rag and bone" man delivered something secretly to our house. It was just after the curfew hours were over. It could have been one of the cows or some wheat. Our father built a threshing machine and he would go to the farms and thresh the wheat. He would arrive home dusty and dirty. The miracle was that none of them, my father included, was ever discovered.

I have absolutely no idea what a "rag and bone" man is or who he was. He had this old crumbling wooden cart and a skinny horse; yes, they were hungry too! He sat hunched over holding the reins and they were both a pretty sad sight. He slipped away in the early morning hours. The poor old man was wrapped in rags and deep in thought. I suspect that he cared little for his safety and had only contempt for the Germans. Maybe the old man had little to lose except his horse and his cart. Perhaps he looked too falling apart for the Germans to stop and question him. The butcher took an enormous risk also because sawing the bones and chopping the meat

42

were not exactly quiet operations. When a family is hungry, desperate measures are taken.

A major upheaval and event came about September of 1942. An order was issued from higher authorities (Hitler) that all residents not born in the Channel Islands be deported to Germany. This was a reprisal because the British government detained German citizens living in Iran. This came as a terrible shock to the Islanders who knew nothing about events in Iran, and for that matter, of the outside world. Pamela, my closest friend at Mandalay school from kindergarten, was born in the town of Taunton in the county of Somerset that is located in the southwest of England. Pam and her family were deported to a camp in Biberach in Germany. I had known her forever or so it seemed and we were inseparable. There was little or no notice and the order was effective almost immediately. It was all so rushed there was a problem in Germany preparing the camps for them.

The news was devastating to the Jersey people and grossly unfair. The Bailiff and civilian government protested vigorously to no avail. We collected clothing and I especially remember that we gave a pair of long johns for Pam's father. I have no idea where they came from, but I do remember thinking that these were the strangest things that I ever saw! As the boat sailed out of the harbor, a large group of onlookers joined them from the shore singing "There'll always be an England." My friend Pam and I did not meet again for many years. We both agree that we are the oldest of friends.

I suppose that the monotony of those years dragged on. One rainy cold night my father was ordered to do guard duty because a cable had been sabotaged. I do not know where this occurred. We just followed orders. He went off with an umbrella and the other men marveled at his presence of mind. They sloshed about all night in a muddy field. Turned out that a cow had bitten into the cable and it was not sabotage after all!

Another incident involved the confiscated wireless sets (radios) which were stored in the parish halls. Jersey is divided into 12 parishes. We lived in the parish of St. Clement. I do not remember the reason for the order, but the men of the parish were ordered by the German authorities to guard these wireless sets. When it was my father's turn for guard duty (it was during the night hours) he hooked up a set and the men had a great guard duty that night. They were able to listen to news of the war from the BBC. Sounds simple, but he was a master of innovation and also creative and brave.

I remember him as an honest man, a Jerseyman who loved his Island and his family above all else. Had he lived, the family would never have left Jersey. He died of cancer in 1952, which was much too young. The undertaker had to bring two hearses for the funeral. One for him and the other for the overflow of floral tributes. My father was well respected in the Island and he and my mother were very happy. It was his death and deep grief that brought her to the US to visit her family who had emigrated after World War 1.

Truth is they, like so many of their generation, were smokers. During the Occupation he grew tobacco, dried it, and smoked it. I never blame that generation, although their coughing should have told them something of the effects of this habit. My mother eventually quit smoking in 1962 and lived to be 90 years of age. My sister and I have never smoked and we consistently refused to empty the ashtrays. None of Anne's children have ever smoked. Education and medical advances make slow but steady progress. I do wonder now about the future and fear for the people in the countries where smoking is still acceptable and encouraged as a commercial enterprise.

Back to the Occupation. It became obvious that I needed a change of school. My parents made arrangements and I became a pupil at the Jersey College for Girls, that had smaller classes and a much more comfortable environment. I have purposely not mentioned the other school by name. My personal experience and feelings about it were and will remain mine. I believe that this should not reflect on the school, but I never missed it.

Uniforms were a big problem. At first I had to wear the one that I already had; there were no new clothes to purchase. This was not "cool" as the kids would say now. It made me different and although we were not called teenagers in those days, being different wasn't in and I intercepted less than kind glances at first. Gradually I happily assimilated and was accepted. The friend I mentioned previously who had only eaten carrots was also a neighbor. We were able to barter some food for one of her old, worn uniforms and that was the most precious piece of clothing I have ever worn! I was very happy for the rest of my school years.

Voisons Department Store, or shop, as we would have described it, was an old established Jersey business. It was a part of our childhood. As children our coats, hats, and clothing were purchased at Voisin's. The brand name for this clothing was Beau Brummel. Apparently the notion of brand names counted even that many years ago. Beau Brummel clothing was recognizable and of very good quality. At Voisins there was another reason that made them special: Miss Le Gros. She was the saleslady in that department. I can see her now as I write. She might be described as a faithful retainer at Voisins. She dressed in the style of the 1920s. She was a rather old fashioned lady. Her demeanor was gentle and soft. She smiled and was the antithesis of the super saleslady.

Voisins has a wonderful staircase. The children's department was on the upper level. That is where our school uniforms were purchased. On a return visit to the Island in 1995, Anne and I went up the staircase to that same department and bought ourselves a school blazer. This was no simple purchase. The saleslady was appalled. Here we were two middle-aged ladies asking to purchase school blazers. In a firm voice she said "You cannot wear them here." Business is business, and reluctantly she packed them up for us. We reassured her and explained that we live in a desert and neither own nor need a winter coat. A blazer would be perfect for our kind of winter. I suspect that she had a great story to tell about this sale. Perhaps the most original of her career. The manufacturer of our blazers was Beau Brummel! Some things never change.

I am also the caretaker of the family pram that my mother bought at Le Gallais, another old Jersey shop. It arrived in Michigan the day before my niece Sheila was born which, as of this writing, is exactly forty years ago. Happy Birthday, Sheila. Great timing Anne! It has been used by all five of Anne's children (including the twins) and the three grandchildren. The brand name is Vesta and it has a beautiful canopy. Fair to say it is in mint condition. Date of purchase was October 5, 1959.

Household chores became more complicated with each month that passed. Mother spent all of her time finding and preparing food. We had the chickens and to this day I am not a chicken enthusiast. We had eggs as I mentioned earlier and these were currency in the barter system. Sometime toward the end of the Occupation, perhaps it was Christmas time, the Germans commandeered chickens for the troops. We sent one scrawny chicken and it probably was tough. He never had feathers on his neck. Questions come into my mind constantly. What, I wonder, did the chickens have to eat?

We hid our wireless in the piano. It was an upright model with a removable panel. Anne was thought to be too young to be told. Doesn't sound so original now and we were certainly not the only family to do this. The piano was also the source of stress because both of us had piano lessons. The teacher was an accomplished classical musician. It was unpleasant for all of us and the torture eventually was discontinued.

If I could choose one special gift now it would be the gift of music. Anne has a beautiful voice, but I was missed on those genes. The best I can do is lip sinc. I enjoy music very much but the notes stop there. I wish that I could play the piano. That is a gift indeed.

Our house was searched twice, but I can only remember the details of one of these invasions of our privacy. I am not sure of the reason for either search and the German police arrived unannounced. My sister and I were separated from our parents, who were taken upstairs. We were shut in the front room. Every drawer was opened but they did not find what they wanted and I am not sure that we ever found out the reason for the search. The encounter left us all shaken but relieved that they had not found the crystal set which Mother had hidden in the oven. The crystal set was used in place of the wireless. It was much easier to hide and a great asset   when the electricity use was restricted. German officers occupied some of the houses that had been left empty by the owners when they evacuated in 1940. A German naval officer lived two doors from us. It may have involved him and his driver, who was a member of the Organization Todt. I do not believe that we ever knew what either of these men actually did for work. We had no contact with either of them. I do remember the neighbors talking about the "ladies" who were the officer's regular visitors but did not understand the purpose of the visits. He was a short little fellow whose uniform coat was long, reaching down to his feet. The memory I have was that his cap was too big for his head.

His driver wore the uniform of the Todt Organization that was a kind of an orange-brown color. This was an organization founded by a Dr. Fritz Todt, who was as convinced as Hitler that the Islands must remain German forever. The organization was founded before the war to direct civilian labor and it assisted the army in building the fortifications along the Western coastline. Under Todt's orders, thousands of foreign workers poured into the Islands. Todt died in 1942 and was succeeded by Albert Speer. Thousands of slave laborers in appalling health and terrible living conditions were forced to build concrete fortifications all around the coastline. They were housed in what were concentration camps. The island of Alderney, emptied of the civilian population was just that. The islanders had been evacuated before the Occupation. I believe that a few of the residents had refused to leave. We had no contact with any of the other islands but most of them can be seen on the horizon from Jersey. Alderney is the most northerly of all of them and I believe that it was deemed wise to evacuate the residents because of its close proximity to Normandy.

These poor multi-ethnic groups from all over Europe were treated worse than animals and suffered brutal treatment from their guards. Many of these were Russian prisoners, some of who escaped and were sheltered by Jersey families. I do not believe that I knew all of these details at the time but I clearly knew that those in the Todt uniform were "bad guys."

One day we were with our parents coming back from a farm where we had purchased some food. At least I think that was the purpose for our journey. We were a long way from home and it was a summer day. We were in a valley and we came upon a German officer holding a mallet. He was knocking the rocks with the mallet. The rock formation was made of Jersey granite. He was diligently going about his task and appeared to be oblivious to us. We thought it was pretty strange and forever afterward referred to him as the rock knocker. His work was not simple at all. After the war underground tunnels were discovered in which a state of the art hospital for those times was discovered. It was built on the backs and with the sweat of slave labor. Today it is a museum and a memorial to those workers.

We lived confident of victory but with no idea when all this would come to an end. News did get through via the very active grapevine. The Allies dropped some leaflets and some came into civilian hands. To be found with one was to invite severe punishment. Dad would always seem to know the war news. The African campaign was encouraging. I can hear him telling my mother that the troops (must have been the British) were closing in on Benghazi in Africa.

We certainly knew when the Americans came in to help us, but I am not sure that there was much talk about Pearl Harbor. Of course this may have been lost on me because I was only 13 or 14 years old and I am sure that I knew nothing of Pearl Harbor. When the Italians were defeated someone cycled past my father and called out, "You won't get anymore macaroni." There was a small contingent of Italian troops in Jersey. The outstanding memory of these men is that they were very small men with unusual hats. They also had a feather with something like a brush in them and the Germans did not regard them as very good fighters.

School continued and that developed some kind of a normal routine. We were approaching the time that we needed to prepare for the final examination, "The Oxford and Cambridge Schools Examination Board School Certificate."

I have often wondered how the teachers coped. I suspect some of them were filling in and teaching subjects that were formerly taught by colleagues who had evacuated. I believe that they were true to their profession and I am grateful to them even today. When we were finally free we took the examinations and we were all successful!

When the Germans arrived they were proud and probably arrogant, young men. This changed over time; the Russian front was taking its toll. The army had taken more than one-half of the Cleveland Garages and a young soldier had started talking to my father. He was fond of talking about his family and was due to go on leave. My father would tell him, "Germany kaput," but young Walter would have none of it. He said he would bring sugar back and he was longing to see his family. He did return and he had a tragic story. He was unable to find his family, but he learned that his younger brother, a university student, had caused some trouble and was shot. He was totally devastated. And of course there was no sugar. Shortly after his return he was ordered to Russia. My father said,"Walter will die, he has no will to live." He always said that Walter was just a kid.

The weekly rations continued to decrease and as long as we had electricity, the hours of usage were curtailed. Soup kitchens had been instituted from the beginning. Also, families could take food to the bakeries where the food was put in the ovens. We never did this, but many families were grateful for this cooking opportunity. Individual families made hay boxes and these worked well. Medicines were almost nonexistent. Doctors made house call on bicycles. When the tires wore out, watering hoses were substituted. Substitute was the word during those years.

A familiar and recurring sight was Mother darning our socks. Knitted cardigans were unraveled and made into new ones. Anne was in the growing stage and she now tells me how uncomfortable it was to walk on darned socks. She, like many children, had only wooden sabots (clogs) for shoes and she set the all-time record for wearing them out. I, on the other hand, had stopped growing and confounded all the predictions that I was going to be a tall person. I do remember begging my mother to barter eggs for a pair of patent leather shoes. I do not remember who made the exchange and they were too big for me, but I was determined and stuffed paper in the toes.

I wish that I could remember what we did for recreation. Our playground had been the beach in the summer time and Jersey has some spectacular coastline. Before the war we were picnic people. Dad would check which way the wind was blowing and choose a bay that was sheltered. Mother packed tea, a selection of sandwiches, cucumber, tomato, egg, etc, and of course cakes. Hot tea in a Thermos flask completed the menu. We had the sea to amuse us and it was fun to explore the rocks. Undressing on the beach was no problem and that was normal procedure. All one needed to do was wrap a towel around oneself and it was done. My aunt and uncle in Michigan took me to a lake in Canada soon after I arrived in the US. I remember their horrified expressions when they saw me change into my swimsuit. They explained that I could be arrested. I can say with absolute certainty that if I were in Jersey I would not hesitate to change into my swimsuit in the traditional way. That is if I would dare to be seen in a swimsuit in public now! It really is easy and no one would take any notice. I often think of those wonderful picnics and wish that I were able to spend a summer afternoon that way again.

Before the war, fish was an important part of our dietary regime and we all enjoyed it; even as small children we ate it and of course we had some that we liked more than others. Naturally, it was fresh from the sea, with the exception of Kippers and Finan Haddie from the UK. Special favorites are hard to find, but here are some of the wonderful choices found in the Island waters. Plaice (similar to sole), lobster, shrimp, spider crab (Jersey only), conger eel, mackerel, etc. Jersey Ormers were considered a delicacy. I believe that they are similar to Abalone. Ormers are only harvested from the rocks in the spring under specific conditions; the ebb and flow of the tide is much greater than usual. This is described as a *Neap* tide when Ormers are found on the rocks many miles out.

The shells have Mother of Pearl lining, which may be where the likeness to Abalone comes from and, when cooked, they have a very distinct odor. My father and Anne loved them. I was ready to move out because the odor was not pleasing to my nose. Luckily, my mother shared my feelings and we must have eaten something else. My Aunt Rita often cooked them for us so I am guessing that these delicacies were popular in the Le Sueur household.

It is surprising how many blanks remain in my mind from 1940 to 1944, but try as I might I cannot distinguish one of those years from the other. Life was relatively simple. School was difficult in the winter as the fuel supplies became more and more scarce. Electricity was rationed and only allowed on for specific hours during the day. I clearly remember the chilblains on my fingers. This is quite painful. The skin over the knuckles would be dry, crack, and bleed. Again knitting came to the rescue and we wore gloves specially made to cover the finger but were open at the fingertips. I am guessing that this condition was caused by the lack of fat in the diet.

I am continually amazed at our endurance and patience because during that first four years we saw no end in sight even though it never occurred to anyone to doubt that victory would come. Curfew and the blackout meant we were confined to our homes during the evening and night hours. There was an official list by the front door in every house listing the occupants.

There was very little to amuse us. One day I found an advertisement in a pre-war magazine for a pair of red shoes with a wedge heel. This was new. I cannot count the times I looked at the picture of those shoes.After the war my mother took me to Beghin's shoe store (another tradition) and we found a green pair exactly the same. I was at the London Hospital Nursing School by then and classmates still remember my green shoes with wedge heels and how much I loved them. They were very comfortable. So many memories and they are such comfortable companions.

We did manage to get news through the crystal set (which we still have today). My mother's family lived in Detroit, Michigan, and she had only received one Red Cross message from them, which gave very little information. Her mother had died, but the family must have decided to hold off with that information until the war was over. Anne and I grew up without grandparents. My father's mother had died very suddenly when I was six months old. Her death was no doubt from a pulmonary embolism. She had been diagnosed with phlebitis. She got up to go to the bathroom and dropped dead. Now I understand the reason for her death, but it was a shock to the family. I missed not knowing her, but I know that she loved me and that she held me in her arms the afternoon before she died. My paternal grandfather died of cancer when our father was nine years old and, yes, he was a smoker. My maternal grandfather died after the war and incredibly when I worked at Bon Secours Hospital in Grosse Pointe, Michigan, some of the Sisters remembered him. Small world.

My father's family was Protestant and my mother's family was Catholic. Both sides of each family were pillars of their faith. The prejudice and misinformation of the times were significant, but Anne and I grew up with two parents who were devoted to one another.

Back to the Occupation, June 1944 is fixed in my memory forever. I began to hear strange things on the crystal set. What was a jeep? Swinging on a star? I used to hide behind a big armchair in the dining room to listen to the news. The hiding place for this crystal set was in the oven. The Germans were showing signs of uneasiness and we were waiting and wondering.

The month of June began with rotten weather. The seas were rough. We had gale force winds and it was wet and cold. June 1 was my birthday but once again no memory of that day. The early morning of June 6th all hell broke loose. Planes flew overhead all night and sleep was impossible. It was happening, *Freedom* was just a few miles away. The Germans responded with anti-aircraft fire. The sky was black with airplanes overhead. The whole island shook and the flash of gunfire was easily seen from the coast.

This was *D-Day*. The Germans issued a proclamation and the Jersey people read in no uncertain terms that aiding the enemy was *Verboten*.

The euphoria and the expectation of liberation went on for hours, days, and weeks. The Islands were to be isolated and there was no plan to attack the German forces. Rather, the plans were to cut them off completely. I can still feel the intense disappointment and the let down as we began to realize our future. It never occurred to me that liberation would be marked with violence. We were destined for a very long and difficult wait. If the Islands had been attacked in June of 1944, many of us would have been killed in the process. What amazes me now is that all I thought of was being free and I was oblivious of the killing and suffering of the invading troops. This is even more troubling to me today because many of those veterans are my friends and their stories now coming to light are awesome. They were not much older than I was at the time. I have thanked them over and over again.

I am diligently attempting to write this story strictly from memory as our family lived it. I know a lot more about the Occupation now thanks to the wonderful authors and the large collection of books on the subject.

As the months wore on, survival became the center of our thoughts and lives. I cannot honestly say that I fully understood the danger we faced because our parents protected us. They were hungry but never let us see that. As the food supply dwindled, our survival was in question. Each Tuesday after school I would cycle up to farmer friends for a bottle of milk. The return journey was all downhill. Nowadays, forgetting milk at the supermarket means all one has to do is hop in the car and go and buy it. We should never take freedom for granted.

There was talk of the possibility that we would receive Red Cross parcels and the anticipation grew as Christmas 1944 approached. It was not to be, but when we finally received one there was never a parcel like that before or after. The Red Cross ship named the Vega arrived December 30, 1944. The parcels were

53

distributed to the public January 4, 1945. The allocation was one parcel per person. The excitement was intense and each one of us opened our parcel so that we could all have the pleasure of finding the contents. They were Canadian and we found real tea, Spam, and corned beef. Sugar and chocolate are some of the items I remember. The weather was unusually cold that year. School was cancelled for about one month because there was no way to heat the classrooms. I imagine we were given plenty of homework.

We were using paraffin lamps for lighting and I do remember supplies were very difficult to obtain. Everything was difficult. The shops had been empty for months. For some reason, deep within me I have always found it difficult to explain to others that empty was empty. In the western world people have difficulty visualizing this fact.

As the Allied forces fought their way through Normandy, some of them were captured and imprisoned in the town of St. Malo in Brittany. There was a German hospital in the town and some of the Allied prisoners who were wounded were held there. When it became obvious that St. Malo would fall into Allied hands the Germans shipped some of the injured American troops to Jersey. Some of them were wounded and they were treated in the General Hospital in Jersey. The Germans had commandeered a section of the hospital early in the Occupation. When the Allied troops were admitted, a German physician, who was a dedicated Nazi, treated them. Considering the supplies that he had at his disposal, he was a skilled physician. Of note is there were no medications. For example, Bob Hanson from South Dakota who was burned to a crisp, described to me how the doctor would debride the dead skin from his eyelids and how he, Bob, would faint each time. The doctor reassured him that fainting produced a morphine-like effect and lessened the pain. After the war, this doctor wrote to Bob and begged for money and asylum in America. Bob was very surprised and he had no money to send this man. That proved to be irrelevant because the US government forbade asylum to this man. Bob Hanson did make an incredible recovery and there is no trace of the scars on his face or hands today. It is interesting to imagine how successful this physician would have been if he had been worthy to enter the United States. His devotion to the Fuhrer poisoned his life and he paid for it.

We would see the Americans marching from time to time but no contact was allowed. It was a big thrill just to see them and I hope they felt our good thoughts. Local people did their best to share food with them. Two of them escaped in January 1945 and passed close to our house before finding shelter with very courageous Jersey families. They escaped to France in a small boat under horrendous sea and weather conditions. Both of these fine men have documented their experience and their stories are awesome.

In 1995, I had the privilege of meeting many of them at their reunion in Jersey. I talk about this later in the book.

The spring of 1945 was difficult from the food point of view, but everyone sensed the day of Liberation was near. Then I heard on the crystal set that we would be free in a matter of days. My Father had the Union Jack flag ready. Wireless sets appeared like magic and finally Winston Churchill spoke to the nation and to all of us in the Channel Islands at 3 p.m. on May 8. He said, "Our dear Channel Islands will be free today." We had been asked by the Bailiff to remain calm and refrain from demonstrations toward the German forces. This we did, but the rejoicing in our homes is beyond describing. I finally was free of the drudgery of putting up those blackout blinds!

The German troops were ordered to remain in their billets and we waited for the British. Admiral Huffmeier, the Naval commander, a dedicated Nazi and devoted to the Fuhrer, had other ideas. He refused to surrender. We went to bed that night still waiting but very happy. The next day we woke up and felt so different. Anne, my father, and I walked up the road to the seawall looking for the British ships to arrive. We saw none on the horizon because Admiral Huffmeir, who was stationed in Guernsey, refused to surrender the Islands. He threatened to fire on the Allied ships. He did not surrender until the next day, May 9, 1945. The next day, we walked up to the sea wall and there they were the British war ships and freedom. We were at the harbor as the first troops arrived. The first person to arrive was a naval officer. In 1995, I met him at one of the Liberation celebrations. His name was Commander Ronald McDonald. He is a surgeon and his medical school was the London Hospital!

Writing about the Occupation years has been difficult. I have deliberately relied on my own memory apart from checking dates and names from time to time. The memories that I have recorded are mine and they will last a lifetime. In a sense, they are written as a gift to my nieces and my nephew. I have recorded them honestly and at times it has been a painful process. I feel compelled to stress that my parents and the majority of the Jersey people conducted themselves during those difficult years with courage and dignity. Their resources were stretched to the breaking point. They were true patriots who believed in victory. They never considered giving up nor did they consort with the enemy. I am proud to be a child of that generation, of Jersey parents, and to be able to say that I was born a Channel Islander.

What did growing up in the Occupation teach me and how did it shape my life? I learned that freedom is not cheap and that most often sacrifice is the price. I learned that the will to endure is in all of us and that only some of us are put to the test. Those lessons learned help form character and last a lifetime. I learned that any other alternative would have been unthinkable. I learned that the love of home and the deep feeling that I have for Jersey are a part of me forever. I learned that life is unpredictable and that we should never stop trying. Finally, I learned that I have been a very fortunate individual and that I would not change one single moment. I know that at any age in our lives the future has endless possibilities.

LIBERATION MAY 9, 1945

The day dawned to a clear blue sky and we were up early. First order of the day was to go to the beach to see if the British ships were on the horizon. When we saw them we dashed home eager to get down to the harbor to greet them. The weather was spectacular and so different from D-Day. We joined a large crowd of very happy people. The troops arrived and it was such a sight to see those British uniforms again. We were in front of the Pomme D'or Hotel and as the crowd spontaneously burst into singing "God Save the King." I noticed a German officer, who had been standing in a window of the hotel, close it and turn away. Presumably he became a prisoner shortly afterwards.

We were wondering if any of our American cousins would be part of the Liberation forces but that was not to be. The day went on and it was very hot. One memory is that we ate well that day. We had boiled Jersey new potatoes for breakfast, dinner, and tea. That was the only food that we had in the house. The reader, unless from Jersey, cannot appreciate the glorious taste and, to tell the truth, I would not refuse such a meal today.

Five long years had changed our lives and children such as Anne had no memory of life in peacetime. Again the next few days are blurred. We went back to school. Communications with the mainland were restored and news started to filter in. The German troops were disciplined and made no attempt to interfere with the Islanders. Perhaps they were happy that it was over and although they faced life as POWs they at least were alive and were fed. They were transported from the Island in incredible ships (LSTs) which opened up before our eyes. The sight amazed us. Supplies began to pour in and at first individuals necessary for priority services began to arrive in the Island. We learned that our former next door neighbor who had evacuated had been killed in an air raid in England. We learned many more wartime stories. Eventually old friends returned and the reunions were wonderful.

At school, my classmates and I were seniors and our school lives would end in July. First, there were the final examinations. I missed out on some of the celebrations to swat (study) for the exams. They were sent over from England and we took our exams in a great room at Victoria College (boy's equivalent of the Girl's College). The girl's school had been occupied by the Germans, so we had been housed in the Preparatory Boy's School building. I was never a pupil in the actual girl's school building, which was a disappointment.

Dr. Evans kept his word and as soon as possible wrote to the London Hospital and recommended me as a candidate for the nursing school. He had qualified at the London Medical School and I was one of the first babies he delivered when he came to the Island as a young physician. I had wanted to be a nurse since I was a small girl. This career choice came to me at the time when little girl's noses begin to change. I think that I was seven or eight years old and I liked my little nose better. I remember that quite clearly.

My first ambition was to be a waitress at Gaudin's tea room. The object of my affection was the custard horns, meringues, and the other marvellous pastries. I also liked the uniform that the waitresses wore and in which I would not be seen dead in today. Looking back, they were very ugly, and they wore black stockings. God is good and he set me straight; I chose nursing.

I was very fortunate to be accepted at the London and I learned that there was a waiting list. I entered with girls that had waited for two years. The London teaching schools were exceptional institutions and the London was respected worldwide. Some of my fellow students remain close friends today. Air traffic was gradually being restored and I flew to England in a small seven-seat plane in September 1945. We arrived in Croydon, Surrey, and the first person I saw when I landed was a German officer walking in front of me. Who he was and where he was going I do not know to this day. I could not believe my eyes! Friends of my parents met me at the airport and I was in a strange country; England. I think that the first Sunday away from home was the loneliest day of my life. What I did not know was that this was separation from the family and the beginning of adulthood: responsibility for oneself and independence. It was quite a painful process, but that is life.

I need to say something about the aftermath of the Occupation. So many of us thought that life would return to normal. What is normal? The old days were gone and we had been forever changed. Other Islanders who had evacuated had also been changed by their experiences. Some who returned to homes they had so hastily fled, found others in them. Some were more fortunate than others in this respect. There were marital upsets and with no divorce allowed by Jersey law, it must have been extremely difficult. The Island had to be cleared of mines; gun emplacements had to be dismantled. Remember, we had been the most fortified coastlines of the Western Wall. The German soldiers were put to work clearing the mines and, fortunately, some had secretly kept plans when originally placing the mines, realizing that they would be reaping what they had sowed.

What I am trying to say is that adjusting to recovery is almost as difficult as it is to become captive. So often in present times that fact is not understood. For example, the fall of the Berlin Wall. As I write this, Yugoslavia is in turmoil and once again because of one despicable individual - a dictator. When our ordeal ended, I thought that nothing like Hitler could ever happen again.

Some days have passed since I wrote the previous lines and I have been left with a sense that I failed to describe the indescribable. To be free after so many years; how does one explain the feeling so that others may understand? I fear that others may read this and think that I want sympathy or that I have exaggerated the Occupation. I believe that thanks to two good people, my parents, I got off pretty lightly. For five years we coexisted and in a sense we got used to living that life. Certainly I did not realize how close we were to starvation and death. Perhaps my parents understood, and, if that is true, what a burden for them.

Always impulsive, today I called the daughter of Mrs. Benton, our principal and owner of Mandalay School. She was surprised, but I wanted her to know how much the school meant to me. It is never too late to say, "thank you." I learned more about the school, and the famous front gate is made of Australian teak and the owner told the Bentons, "If you don't take care of it I will haunt you." Others and I walked through that wonderful gate for many years. When the school was demolished, it was left as a reminder of a special place where so many of us learned our first lessons.

*Father after the war,
approximately 1947.*

Sheila with a Jersey calf. June 1947.

*Pauline (O'Flaherty) Campbell
and Sheila in Guernsey in 1947.*

CHAPTER FOUR

The London Hospital

The month of August was spent in great anticipation as I prepared to go to England and the London Hospital for my nursing education. My application had been tentatively accepted. I completed all the prerequisites including the physical examination and chest x-ray, although I have no memory of either of these now. I do remember taking the examination for the Oxford and Cambridge school leaving certificate which was sent over to the Island as a priority. The results had not yet arrived so it seems that allowances were made for this unusual circumstance. The final step was a personal interview with Miss Alexander, the Matron. The prospectus had arrived and I pored over it for hours. I chuckle over this now because I had no idea what work was and it was much, much later that it dawned on me that I had to earn my living. I felt that I had only two options: to be a teacher or a nurse and my mind had been made up for a long time. Working for a bank was another popular option and in those days there was a certain amount of status in doing that. If eventually I make it to Heaven there are three things that I would hate as an assignment. They are filing, cooking, and balancing the heavenly checkbook. Banking was definitely not for me. Teachers seemed to be old maids and they wore glasses. So I became an unmarried nurse and I wore glasses!

Back to the prospectus. The rules set out were clear and I soon found out, cast in stone. There was a 48-hour week. The initial nine weeks would be spent in the preliminary training school followed by a three-month trial period on the wards. If successfully completed, I would be asked to sign a solemn and binding agreement for three years. The Matron could at any time terminate this agreement if the individual was found to be unsatisfactory. There was the right of appeal to the house committee. Nothing would have stopped me. My father was not in favor of my career choice and would have preferred that I remain in the Island. My mother, who had an opportunity to go to a teacher's college in England denied because her mother thought her health too frail, supported me. She lived to be 90 years of age and would have made a great teacher.

I believe that leaving the Island, going to England and the London, was the bravest decision that I ever made. I had never been comfortable being away from home for even a night and this was probably enhanced by the fact that for five years this would have been impossible. I flew to England unaccompanied in a small plane that only had seats for seven passengers. This modest air service had just been reinstated. Friends of my parents, who lived in New Malden, Surrey, met me and were very kind to me. Auntie Flo, as we called her, took me up to the London for the personal interview and I was accepted for the class or set, as it was known, that was to begin October 15, 1945. We shopped for my black shoes and stockings. They were ugly and the shoes pinched, but the war had just ended and the selection combined with my small feet was not the greatest. I suffered many painful hours in those shoes. We bought, as per listed, bath towels, an eiderdown (comforter), a pair of blunt-ended surgical scissors (I still have them), a fountain pen, a watch with a second hand and a small pocket watch. The black shoes had to be Oxford style with rubber heels. These had to be purchased with my own clothing coupons. This was a step up because all through the Occupation there was nothing to buy for even one coupon! The hospital provided the uniforms and there were plenty of them. We were also provided with dark blue cloaks lined in scarlet except that our set had blue lining due to the war. I guess the blue material was more available than the scarlet. The uniform code was strictly enforced and we all had a professional appearance. I believe the relaxed dress code that is permitted now does nothing for the profession. The cloaks were wonderfully comfortable like old friends. Our uniforms did not have the traditional London Hospital puff sleeve, again due to the war. I think our uniforms were attractive and laundry was all done for us at no cost. We received "pocket money" at 40 pounds per year with increments of five pounds each year. We were required to surrender six clothing coupons each year for our uniforms.

I encountered many experiences during the first few weeks before I entered the London. The flight was my first plane ride. Transportation was so different: trains, London buses, the tube (London underground transport) and learning to follow the directions and where to get on and off. Seeing an escalator for the first time and learning to get on and off without losing my balance was a major accomplishment. Freedom was all around me and I pressed on.

The English accent was different and so was the lifestyle. Our friends were Club people and every evening we would walk to the Club. It was probably a golf club, but I only remember the socialization and the lounge. I was persuaded to taste beer and thought it was horrible and have never been tempted since. I enjoyed going to the shops and seeing the shelves stocked with all kinds of food that I had not seen for years. There were no supermarkets in those days. We went to the greengrocer and bakery. The fishmonger was a favorite shop because Auntie Flo made wonderful meals with the fresh fish. There was the newsagent for the paper and magazines. It also sold sweets (candy). Seeing all this after so long was like a miracle. Rationing was in place in England but after the Occupation it all looked plentiful to me. There naturally is no comparison between living in London and in Jersey. By the time I left London, I knew my way around like a native and have retained a fondness for that great city to this day.

My mother had relatives in the famous naval port of Plymouth in Devon. Plymouth is in the southwest of England and I was invited to visit them before starting life at the London. The journey by train was another first and it was a long one - about six hours as I recall. Auntie Flo saw me safely on to the train and this is the absolute truth - I never moved for the entire journey. The other passengers must have thought I had turned to stone. I was really nervous and the train seemed to fly into the unknown.

When the train pulled into Plymouth station, the family was waiting for me. I met new cousins and I had a wonderful time. Everything was new and different. Once again the evening visit to the pub. I did not like this routine. This was part of the social structure and everyone seemed to know everyone else. The drink of choice offered to me this time was a shandy, just as unpleasant as the beer. I never pursued either of these refreshments. This was a total lifestyle change. In Jersey law forbade women to be in the same part of a pub as the men. A separate lounge was provided for them. I am guessing that a waiter took orders and the drinks were served to them. My father was neither a beer drinker nor a public house patron so this was all different to me. I never liked being around cigarette smoke and I did not understand its dangers at that time. It was the odor that I found to be totally obnoxious. To this day I do not enjoy alcohol and that is not a problem.

Summer faded and it was time to return to our friends in Surrey. New Malden is close to London and in those days it was the best that suburbia had to offer. New Malden is in the county of Surrey and it is a beautiful county. Lots of lovely English flowers everywhere. It is about a thirty-minute train ride to London. It is close enough and far enough away from the city. The famous palace of Hampton Court and the Wimbledon tennis courts are nearby and well worth a visit. I enjoyed walking through the maze at Hampton Court. The day arrived and it was time to go to the London.

My father came from Jersey to take me and we went by train to the little village of Ingatestone in Essex. Probationers at the London were referred to as "Tredegears" and housed in Tredegear House, a separate building from the other nurses' residences, at the London. Tredegear House had been bombed before the end of the war and had not been repaired when our set arrived for training. We were lucky, we were assigned to a country estate. We were sent to a beautiful old country mansion named "Trueloves." It was situated in the Essex countryside. I met new friends and we had fun. The train that we travelled on was what might be called a puddle jumper and it stopped at every station.

Our compartment was still out on the tracks when the train slowly pulled into the tiny railway station. We eventually got off and started up a winding hill. I do not remember luggage, but I noticed another girl with an unusual bike. It was an American bike and her clothes were different. She was wearing penny loafers and I spotted them right away. Actually, she was English, but her father was posted in Washington, DC. She used to go to America for her holidays and I thought that was awesome. Some years later, after I'd settled in America, I saw her at a reunion in England and she told me that I spoke with an accent just as she had done!

Two London Hospital sister tutors greeted us at the door. They were Miss Kay and Miss Norway. Miss Norway had a small gray poodle named Penny and I was immediately attracted to him. Penny was unimpressed. He had seen many more of the likes of me. I was assigned alphabetically to a five-bed room with the other Ls. I chose my spot but Dad did not think that I made the right choice. It was fine. What was not was the fact that my mother had insisted that I wear my money tucked in a little pouch in my bra. Bedtime brought gales of laughter when I removed my money and that was the end of that!

Remember that I was from a small island fresh from the Occupation and the London was in Jack the Ripper country. Jack the Ripper preyed on and disemboweled prostitutes in the East End of London long before I arrived on the scene. His identity has never been revealed, but there were rumors he belonged to an aristocratic family. The legend is that only the family physician knew Jack's real identity and he died with the secret some years later.

We had classroom studies and learned bed making, and horror of horrors, invalid cooking. Many of my classmates could cook and even if I had been interested during the Occupation there was nothing to spare or waste so I simply had no opportunity and eventually there was no fuel for the stoves. So that is to what I attribute my total lack of interest in learning the culinary arts.

Most girls were able to go home for the weekend. Little did they know that it would be their last for years! All through training, we never had a weekend off and what is worse, it never occurred to us that we should! I do not remember anyone complaining about this.

One of our classes was named "housewifery" and we cleaned Trueloves from top to bottom! One of the girls wore gloves to do this. She outscored most of us academically, but after only three weeks on the ward at the London she was gone! Forty-three of us survived and successfully completed our final examinations. Probably about five of those who started dropped out. I consider this a great accomplishment and of course there were ups and downs along the way.

At Trueloves I met Pauline O' Flaherty. She was assigned to the room two doors down the hall from mine with the Os. I spent the first weekend at Trueloves and soon afterwards Pauline invited me to her home for the weekend.

She and her family were from Kent and this meant two long bus trips to get there. At least, they were long to me. I know that during the journey we had to cross the Thames River. All of this was new and exciting for me. It was a cold and damp November day and we had quite a walk to reach her home. I shall never forget walking in the house and meeting her parents. There was a roaring fire in the fireplace and it was a home where I was accepted as a family member. There were countless happy times in the O'Flaherty home during those years. Pauline was an only child and she had been born in Sydney, Australia, so that made us alike in some respects. She had been evacuated during the war and it was not a good experience. My life during the Occupation had been a lot easier.

We completed our time and we were able to go home for Christmas. I remember that I took my uniform home with me and paraded around to whoever would admire my new outfit. It was at this time that my mother bought me some green wedge heel shoes (just like the red ones that I had pined over in that magazine during the Occupation) and a really nice green coat to go with them. Clothes were just coming back to the Island. I do not remember if we had clothing coupons in Jersey but the supply was probably limited and the demand after so many years was great.

I flew back after Christmas and our set met once again but this time at the London. There were many buildings that covered many blocks. It was totally imposing and in reality I was stepping into history. The London Infirmary was founded as a charity September 23rd. 1740. A group of seven met in the Three Feathers tavern in Cheapside, in the East End of London. A house was leased in Featherstone Street for five years. The purpose was to care for the sick and the ailing. The need was enormous. During the Middle Ages, the care of the sick fell to the monasteries. When Henry VIII severed all ties with Rome because of his marital difficulties, he plundered the religious orders. He needed their money. The destruction meant there simply was no place for the poor to seek care and shelter. By the 1700s the needs were desperate and solutions were beginning to be discussed.

The next priority facing these men was finding staff to care for the patients. Forgive me if I add a personal note here: "some things never change." Mr. John Harrison, a surgeon and one of the seven men, engaged a man and a woman to care for the patients. Staffing continued to be a problem but the Infirmary soon outgrew its capacity. Out of this humble beginning the London Hospital evolved and when I walked into the entrance I was stepping into the largest voluntary hospital in the United Kingdom.

The London Hospital was *History*! My first impression was that the walls in the entrance and surrounding corridors were covered with white shiny and spotlessly clean tiles. At the entrance were the porters and they were a great group of men. On the left wall there was a bell. I learned later that this was used to summon help to hold the patients down during surgery before the days of anesthesia! Impossible to contemplate this now. How grateful we must all be for progress and for those who made things happen in the past. The patients must have been in desperate circumstances to submit themselves to this treatment. I believe that other members of the medical staff held the patients down. In my day, the porters seemed to be able to answer any question and I had the utmost respect for them. The porters did what the transport staff does now. They delivered specimens and that kind of work. To be honest, I remember them best for their cheerful greeting and willingness to help. I confess I was always too worried about what I was doing to pay attention to others. We were assigned to the Luckes Nursing Residence. I was given the ultimate in dreary rooms.

Miss Eva Luckes was appointed Matron in 1880 at the age of twenty-six. She served for almost forty years until her death in 1919. Miss Luckes was a giant in her time. She established the principle that "patients come first" for everyone involved in the hospital and that was no less true during my years there. She pressed for individual responsibility, economy and accountability. It was she who began the first preliminary training school for nurses in England in1895. She wrote textbooks, taught classes and arranged for the nurses to attend lectures given by physicians and surgeons. Consequently, others and I learned from some of the most distinguished members of the medical profession whose work and research is known to this day. In the voluntary hospital system, the attending staff received no fees but maintained private practices elsewhere in the city. I remember seeing some of their names on shiny brass plates on the doorway of houses in Harley Street.

The London was the largest voluntary hospital in the United Kingdom until the 1940s. I clearly remember when that change occurred. It was the start of the National Health Service. Most significant to me at that time was that we no longer wore the black shoes and stockings. My new brown shoes pinched my feet just like the black pair. Obviously nationalized medicine brought about swift and dramatic changes in the delivery of the health care system. It is said of the London that there have always been too many patients and too little money.

When I walked into that great institution, I had no idea or appreciation that I was walking into history, tradition and excellence. All I knew was that Dr. Mortimer Evans, our family Doctor in Jersey had always promised me that I would go to his school. I am startled by the truth that at the age of 18, I missed so much of life around me.

On the other hand, I was forced to play catch up because the war had taken so much from all of us.

Here was I beginning this new experience from the Island of Jersey when less than a year ago my very survival had been in question. Of course, I did not realize it then but I am sure that most of the adults in the Island were acutely aware of our jeopardy.

We each had our own room in the Luckes home and luckily Pauline's was in the same long corridor. We were on the ground floor. My room was not a gorgeous sight. The windows were of frosted glass for privacy. The blanket on the iron bed was the dingiest shade of green. The eiderdown had double duty - the first to keep one warm and the other to cover the hideous blanket. There was a desk, a chair and a corner wardrobe. The toilets and the bathrooms were at the end of the long corridor. The bathtubs had a line painted in them and that was the level of water we were supposed to use. This had been a wartime economy measure. England was just recovering from the wartime horrors such as bombings, the Doodlebugs and V3 silent rocket bombs. The London had suffered considerable bomb damage, and as indicated getting over a war is very, very difficult.

Back to the bathtubs. We took our baths at night, after duty. Whoever made it off duty first made a beeline and started the water running to reserve it for our pals. We worked six days per week from 7a.m. until 8:30 p.m. with three hours off during the morning or afternoon. Night duty was, I think, from 8:30 p.m. until 8:00 a.m. We had an hour off during the night for a meal and I cannot remember tea breaks, but this may have happened. The seniors started the dinner hour at 11 p.m. and it moved down from there. The lowly ones got to wait until 1 a.m. By that time, I was half dead because as long as I have been alive I cannot sleep during the daytime. This was my one enduring agony during my years at the London. There were no exceptions and I am glad that I never quit although I thought about doing that every night. Part of the problem was that we were assigned to night duty for as long as six months at a time. The scheduled days off were two at a time totaling four per month. It did happen that one could have all of these close together and long stretches after that. I never minded the work; it was just that I was exhausted.

My first assignment was on day duty on one of the pediatric wards. It was named Buxton after one of the benefactor families. All of the wards had names; many were after breweries, again benefactors. The London was financed through voluntary contributions.

I remember going on duty each morning that January of 1946. It was dark and I was awakened by the blast of a loud and demanding bell. The senior night sister signed us in for breakfast; no calling in sick in this outfit. She inspected our uniform and clean shoes were mandatory. Pauline, who had all the self confidence I lacked, used to rub her shoes on her black stockings to clean them and passed muster every time. Never got caught. Once I bought a pair of shoes with wedge heels. Sister, who never missed even a minor change in appearance, saw them immediately and I heard about that, but I do not remember the end of this story.

Two other incidents are forever in my mind. I believe the first patient for whom I ever cared was a little girl. I'll call "O". She must have been about 18 months old. She had blonde curly hair. This curly hair was the first challenge of my career. She had a condition known as "Pediculi." For the uninitiated, this is lice. I have my original procedure book and dictionary in front of me as I write, Ballieres Nurses Complete Medical Dictionary, Margaret Hitch, tenth edition, 1943, and I quote: "Pediculosis. The condition of being infested with lice." "O" was such a sweet little girl. The treatment which Sister (I have no memory of who she was) instructed me to apply was a Carbolic cap. I have the written procedure in front of me, but I will spare the reader the technical details. I hope that I made "O" more comfortable because as I remember she gave me no resistance.

The second early memory was of a young boy in a cot (crib) who needed to use the urinal. I must have been instructed in the mysteries of this procedure, but as I started to help the little boy, a wretched medical student appeared on the scene with "What's the matter nurse; don't you know what to do?" If I did, all thought vanished from my mind. I have never fainted in my entire life, but this would have been the perfect time to try. I do not know if this vile creature ever finished medical school, but over the years I have thought of a zillion snappy answers that I could have used. I have even imagined hitting him over the head with the urinal or worse but no description of that would pass the censor now.

The children had tiny ceramic bedpans that were placed in a sterilizer after use. The task of emptying the now sterilized "potties" often fell to me. They were scalding hot and I frequently dropped and broke them. This was not my finest hour and I was reprimanded for my clumsiness. I must have written home about this because a message came back from my father, "Break them and I will pay for them." I doubt that this would have solved the problem and I must have developed the perfect technique because I do not recall any more potty problems.

The final chore at the end of the day shift was washing the woolly booties and little woolly sweaters. Remember I had never before done a day's work and between my aching feet with the too tight shoes and hands that were red and raw from repeated hand washing, I must have really wanted to be a nurse to survive. I loved the children. Now here comes the shocker. Visiting time was *only* after the children were asleep. That is a hair-raiser today.

At the end of three months I was transferred to night duty. I was assigned to the same ward at first but soon after I was transferred to Milward, a women's medical ward. This was a big change from pediatrics. Different diagnoses and caring for adults. I have often thought what a convenient way to recruit night nurses. One of the responsibilities of the junior nurse on night duty was to greet the night Sister (Supervisor) on her 6am round and inform her of the temperature of the ward. I remember dreading this until one morning one of the other nurses gave me a verbal push and said, "she is waiting, go and tell her!" I can see Sister now, waiting for me. I suppose that I went up to her and told her the temperature of the ward. This must have been for tradition purposes only. The young night Sister was Miss Friend now Dame Friend. I have good memories of her. One night, while I was still on pediatrics, I was sent on an errand to one of the medical wards and I caught sight of a very young woman who had just died. Never having seen a dead person before, I got back to Buxton ward and proceeded to vomit non- stop. I was hospitalized in the special ward for sick nurses. We were well cared for and with great kindness. I do not know what the diagnosis was but to this day I think that whatever it was it was caused by my first experience with death. I do remember the benefit of being in the ward for sick nurses was that I was glad to be in a bed at night and for the brief respite from night duty.

After that I was transferred to the very same medical ward named Milward. As I write this I wonder if the transfer was deliberate. Sort of like falling off a horse and having to get up on it again. It was a women's ward. As I remember there were 28 beds divided in two parts, it was like two 14-bed wards and there were two openings or pass-throughs, identified as the "gap" so that is really one ward. There was another ward adjoining it named Paulin. It had a different patient population. Between these was an area known as the lobby. This was the work area, and in it was the linen room, which was very, very tidy, a bathroom, and sterilizers for boiling the instruments. The bathroom was for ambulatory patients to have a bath and shampoo on admission. The hair was combed and examined and, if necessary, combed with a toothcomb. The necessary reason for this being the possible presence of Pediculi. The toothcomb has no connection with the tooth fairy. I must add a comment here. Procedure books are crucial to all nurses and I am checking the facts from my old book that I used some 50 plus years ago. In the present climate, failure to follow procedure would set the practitioner subject to litigation. I have never been involved in such a situation, but I have been a diligent user of the procedure book for my entire nursing career. They are a lifesaver for the nurse and the patient.

Back to the lobby. There was a small room where the medical students and the nurses tested the patients' urine with a Bunsen burner. These had a habit of boiling over the sides of the test tube and the walls of this room had a distinctive odor as I recall. Then there was the holy of holy's the sluice room. I spent a lot of time in there. The London hospital is the *only* institution that I worked in, that ever had accurate fluid charts (intake and output). For one thing, the lowly probationer was not allowed to leave duty until the totals were correct. Another was the convenience of their location. The patients' charts were on a clipboard and hooked on a rail over the bed. The physicians order sheet was clearly visible and we worked from it. The chart was in a folder behind it with the fluid chart right up front. I never found a better system in almost 50 years of practice.

The sluice room was where the dustbins (trashcans) were kept. There was a huge sink and above it rows of ceramic jars with lids. These were known as the SMU'S (saved and measured urine) Presumably this was for the patients on restricted intake or saved for some reason. One of the first assignments each morning was to empty these jars and wash them in disinfectant. The odor was sufficient to guarantee to clear the most severely blocked sinuses. Another duty that coincided with this was boiling the eggs for breakfast. I think all the patients were served eggs for breakfast. I have already described my aversion to cooking and it is not surprising I consistently had difficulty with this task. The SMU'S were a snap by comparison. Another nurse told me to wrap the eggs in gauze and that made them easier to retrieve. I have often wondered how many of those patients had hard-boiled eggs for breakfast.

The patients were so kind to us. These were the East Enders who had survived the blitz. One never to be forgotten night I arrived on duty on Milward, and Sister M. told me that Mrs. B. had died and I was to clean up the area around the bed. Icy fear clutched at my throat. Why did I not tell her that seeing dead people was new to me? I never thought of that and, besides, I was scared of her. Ward Sisters were the supreme leaders of each ward. This was known to all from the bottom to the top and I mean the top. Consultants respected the Sisters and their role absolutely. So that is why I was so timid I suppose.

I found myself at the bedside and promptly tripped over the oxygen tank that was lying on the floor. Finally, I finished the job, but I have never forgotten this lady. I never knew her alive so she must have been admitted and died shortly thereafter. I know her name and the diagnosis. It is forever etched in my mind. She was a small woman and had bright red fingernails. Presumably the porters carried Mrs. B. away. Next task was to set up the breakfast trays in the lobby. Another of my set, Evelyn W. shared this task. She, like me, was the probationer in the adjoining ward. I cried and cried and I swore that I was going home in the morning! I did not.

All was well until midnight when night Sister came looking for Mrs. B.'s dentures. "No problem," I said to myself, wondering why a dead lady needed teeth. I retrieved them swiftly from the dirty wool trash bin and carried them out safely with a pair of Cheatle forceps to the now horrified Sister.

I get ahead of myself. Another great feature of patient care at the London was that we never used toilet paper for the patients. Gray wool, a little more consistent than cotton wool, was used and this was much more comfortable for the patients. The Cheatle forceps were for disposing the soiled material into the dustbin known as the dirty wool bin. By now the reader will have guessed where I had deposited the teeth. Honestly, Sister's wrath was something to behold.

This time I really was going home in the morning. I did not! I must have been the story of the night and I sure hope that someone saw the funny side of it. I had an opportunity to talk with this Sister at the London Hospital League Day in 1995 and she assured me that she had had a "titter" over it. This Sister was not much older than I was, but I had no concept of age. They all looked old and wiser to me and they represented authority. Power is awesome. All through my career nurses had trouble with dentures. The wearer of these can be very careless with them. The important lesson I took away from this misadventure was that no nurse was ever directed by me to care for a dying or dead patient without my asking him or her if this was their first experience with death. The London was a teaching hospital and I had learned something that I could use to help other nurses. Thank you Mrs. B.

We wore white aprons over our uniforms and the last duty of the night was to clean the inkwells on Sister's desk. All that I can say about this is that I consistently had the most patriotic aprons ever to enhance the London hospital uniform: red, white and blue.

One other duty that must be mentioned was making the toast for breakfast. This was done before the patients were awakened. I had grown up with an Aga cooker- no flame and no matches. In the hospital kitchens, I found enormous service-type stoves and matches. These stoves or ovens lit with a bang and I often jumped so hard out went the flame. I used a lot of matches. Why, I wonder as I write this, did I need an oven to make toast? I have no idea. I am a great supporter of cold toast. I have it for breakfast every morning. Prepared in a toaster I hasten to add!

I have spoken about how we all dashed for the bathrooms after duty. There were many nurses housed in each corridor. My room became the gathering place after duty. We were always hungry and my mother kept us going with food parcels from home. We gave detailed descriptions of the horrors of the day and laughed a lot. My aunt in Michigan sent me a package with tea bags in it. We had never seen anything but loose tea so this was a novelty.

This gathering of classmates was on the day duty; on nights, everyone just went to bed. Pauline and I enjoyed shop gazing, which is exactly all we could afford to do. We had three hours off each day and most often mornings we would dash up to the West End of London walk up and down Bond Street and dash back again for duty. If our days off coincided we went to Kent where Pauline's mother waited on us with wonderful meals like breakfast in bed. We managed to get up for dinner and tea before it was time to go back to London.

The nursing staff was under the direction of Miss Clare Alexander, who was the leader in the nursing profession in the UK if not in the world at that time. An LH nurse, it was said all over the world, "epitomized the essence of the hospital." In other words, they were top notch. I know that medical colleagues all over the world had confidence in and sincere respect for an LH nurse. It was said that an LH nurse could go anywhere to work and at one time not even a reference was necessary.

Miss Alexander changed the term probationer to student nurse. We were instructed by Sister tutors in the classroom and by the ward Sisters in the clinical setting. The London housed many schools for other disciplines including the Medical and Dental colleges. There were Radiography, Physiotherapy students, Lady Almoners (social work), Dietary, etc. I must remind the reader that the nurses were the only part of this mix that was at the patient's bedside around the clock. This responsibility has never changed. The study day had been instituted when we arrived and this was absolutely wonderful. This was our classroom experience; we wore our civilian clothes and following the day in the classroom were off duty for the next 24 hours at 5 p.m.

Pauline and I were packed and ready to go to her home in Kent. Pauline always had to catch the train just leaving the station and we made one mad dash to catch it.

The consulting staff physicians and surgeons taught us in the classrooms and in the clinical setting. Dr Clarke Kennedy, President of the medical school and author of many books on the London, was my favorite teacher. He had the ability to make complicated concepts simple. He also instructed us at the bedside.

Initially, we were all assigned at the London Hospital in Whitechapel. Now I shall relate my experience at the sector hospitals. During the war and the intense air raids, it became necessary to evacuate patients and some services from London. When our set arrived in 1945 these other hospitals were still in existence. They were scattered all around London in various suburban counties. I was transferred to the Annex at Brentwood in

Essex. This was a series of Quonset huts that accommodated 345 beds. During the war, the sector hospitals freed up the London for casualties in the city. The patient population at the Annex housed medical and surgical patients and specialties such as neurosurgery, gynecology and thoracic surgery. There were 70 other beds provided for patients with tuberculosis. I was never assigned to these because I had a positive Mantoux test. The Mantoux test was given to determine if the individual had ever been exposed to Tuberculosis. The results of my test were not surprising. In the early 1900's tuberculosis was very prevalent in Jersey. Members on both sides of our family had contracted tuberculosis and died from it. The disease had been controlled by the time my generation came along. The bacillus was found in the Jersey milk. A medical officer of health, Dr. Mckinstry, came to Jersey and dedicated himself to eliminating this scourge on Island life and he was as good as his word. He made a great contribution and saved many lives. He looked very much like my father. I remember being at a Christmas party on Boxing Day with my family and one of the little boys burst into terrified tears. He thought his doctor was at the party and he obviously feared an injection was on his way or perhaps some bad tasting medicine.

As I write this, I complicate my story for the American reader and find my self-tripping over words. For the British it must be injection, not shot, and for the Americans I must explain Boxing Day. It was a really fun day in my pre-war childhood. I believe it was a Victorian tradition. Boxing Day follows Christmas Day and it was the day when trades people and servants received boxes (gifts) sort of like the downstairs people from the upstairs people. It was often in the form of a monetary gift for the tradespeople.

For our family and friends, it was a morning to go to the drag hunt and follow the hounds. We of course went as observers by car. The horses and riders would assemble and they would gallop following the hounds jumping over the hedgerows. I do not believe that there are foxes in Jersey, so the prey must have been a rabbit. Anne only has a slight memory of this because all of this ceased with the Occupation. We would go home for cold turkey dinner and all

78

the trimmings. Then it was into party dress, velvet cloaks and off we went to farmer friends to a wonderful Christmas party. This couple had no children but gave all of us a wonderful day, complete with a huge Christmas tree and Father Christmas banging on the window laden with presents. I suppose we had the inevitable Jell-O, Blanca Mange and bread and butter for tea. All of my parents' friends and children were there and it was a wonderfully happy occasion. Such memories are warm in the heart and beyond any price.

Back to the Annex at Brentwood. My first assignment was the male Neuro surgical ward. The London Neuro surgeon, Hugh Cairns, was a pioneer in this field, but he was before my time. Others followed and the work continued. I remember one young patient very clearly. He had a brain tumor and was recovering from surgery. I seem to remember that the tumor was inoperable. He had lost the ability to feed himself. At the London, the nursing staff sat at the patient's bedside when feeding them, not standing as we often see now. To this day I believe that this was good practice. Well, I was feeding F. and all was well until he asked me for something on the plate, which I was avoiding. He said that he liked it and I suddenly realized that I did not. I never forgot this incident and never made that mistake again. Sitting at the bedside was so much more companionable for the patient. Did not Shakespeare write that the company is the sauce for the meat? The food that I was avoiding escapes my memory.

I remember another patient, J. He was a wonderful Cockney from the East End who had been through all of the bombing. I am not sure if he had been in the armed services. He had developed skin disease, something like Pemphigus. This is described in my old dictionary as an acute or chronic skin disease characterized by an eruption of large blebs that leave pigmented areas on healing. Itching may be marked and usually general health is impaired. J. was probably in his thirties and had suffered with this disease for some time. I remember someone telling me that this condition could last for seven years.

I remember this remarkable man with much kindness. He had little of the world's goods, but he was one of nature's gentlemen. Every day we would spend all morning in the bathroom doing his treatment. All of the bandages came off (my memory is not positive about this) and he soaked in the bathtub. Then ointment was applied all over his body. He was very modest and respectful to all of the nurses. It was a long treatment and I always enjoyed talking with him. One day I was scolded for forgetting to collect my pocket money from Matrons' office. I remember how unimportant this seemed to me at the time. I wonder what happened to him. I hope he recovered and had some life; he certainly earned it.

I was assigned to the gynecological ward and I must have been a very junior nurse during my time at the Annex. We students had Blue Books in which were listed all of the skills in which we were required to be proficient. It was my turn to be observed in the procedure of catheterizing a female patient. For the lay person, this was to obtain a sterile urine specimen. I had seen others fail in their attempt so I prepared ahead, or so I thought! The first task was to boil the catheters in the sterilizer. They were removed with sterile forceps and placed in a sterile container. All this, plus sterile towels, were put on a trolley and wheeled to the bedside. Sister and the patient were waiting. So I started following the procedure very carefully. It was time to remove the lid from the metal container, which I did, and there neatly stacked side by side were a dozen or so catheters. Sister nearly exploded and said, "What is this?" The procedure called for two sterile catheters. I replied, "In case I miss." It is a wonder that the patient did not run for cover. Well, we all survived and once again the Sisters' dining room must have heard my name and not in the most flattering of terms.

In 1947, England experienced severe snowstorms. Once again I was on my favorite tour of duty the night shift. We were housed away from the hospital in another stately country home named "Merry Meade." I remember walking through deep snow down what I think was Ongar Road. Our feet were soaking wet and I cannot remember if we had coats or our cloaks. I do remember walking by houses and how I wished I could be warm and cosy and living in them.

The benefit of the Annex was that we could have our bikes and mine was sent over from Jersey. It was good to be able to get out in the country. In the village, there was a pastry shop that sold the most delicious sausage rolls. We would be waiting for it to open and we used our pocket money to feast on these wonderful treats. I never tasted better ones. No one thought of calories or cholesterol in those days. Also, we were all working hard. We used to go up to the London for our class days. The buses were double-deckers and not heated. Pauline was at the Annex for part of the time with me and we made the same trip to her parents over and over again.

We were transferred back to the London and our training was mapped out so that we had an all round experience. We sat for two major examinations: the preliminary, probably at the halfway mark; and the final, which qualified us as State Registered Nurses. The format was in three parts. There was a practical examination in which we demonstrated competence in procedures, the oral, and the written.

I particularly remember the oral in the final exam. A physician was the examiner. I can see the individual who questioned me now. He sat and looked at me with one hand covering his eye with his fingers. He asked me all about venereal disease. As a matter of fact, this was fortunate. Venereal disease was very much a common diagnosis in those days. I had cared for many patients, not in the acute stages of their illness, but with the long-term consequences of the infection. General Paralysis of the Insane was one diagnosis that I clearly remember.

There were many operating theaters at the London and I did my turn. I liked counting the swabs best of all. I was not destined to make this area a career goal. Pauline loved it and went on to make an excellent theater Sister. My discomfort was the huge and heavy trays that one had to lift out of the boiling hot sterilizers and no one seemed to ask for anything; they just looked and expected me to read their mind. On night duty, one of my responsibilities was to clean the surgeons white boots. Feminists would faint at the thought today. This kept me out of harms way and they had to be clean. I shall never forget seeing the surgeons' boots in America. Some of them were disgusting no one cleaned them.

The Orthopedic service at the London was very well known. Sir Reginald Watson Jones had made historic progress in this field of medicine. The prevention of infection was maintained in the most intense manner. The surgeons were double-gowned to cover back and front and they handled all of their instruments with Spencer Wells forceps. The nurses assisted with the gown procedure, also with forceps. The preparation for the operative area was very specific. I shall never forget holding the leg up of an anethetised patient while the surgeon "prepped" the leg. The leg belonged to a very large man and Mr. K., the surgeon, became impatient and said to me "Get on a bloody soap box." The leg was as high as I could lift it and it weighed a ton. Shortly afterward Miss Latham, the Sister in charge, came in and told the surgeon that he would kindly refrain from talking to the student nurses in that manner. Justice! Miss Latham, a legend at the, London represented what we all would want to become. She was firm but fair and even though the operating theater had no appeal to me, I respected her above all of the sisters with whom I worked in the clinical setting.

Later, one of the set that I qualified with, Margaret Kneale Jones, assumed the responsibility and role. She was an incredibly gifted individual and died of cancer too young. The London was privileged to have these two individuals on the staff, and the nurses no less privileged to learn from them.

I remember a big celebration one summer day. Old Londoners visited for the day and it was a happy day. Somehow I managed to eat eight ice creams, I suppose in between working. The next day I had a rash plain for all to see. Home Sister ordered me to the sick room. I was positive that the rash was from the ice cream and I begged her, but she would have none of it. Truth is I had rubella (German measles).

So there was I in the sick nurses ward. Pauline had spent time in there with chicken pox. The consultant who made rounds was Sir Horace Evans, later Lord Evans and physician to the Royal Family. He examined me and said two words, "Not much." When it was time for discharge, I was sent to recover at a convalescent home for orthopedic patients at Banstead, Surrey. This was because my home was in Jersey. Normally, girls would be sent home. Well, Banstead was wonderful and later I was assigned there. It was fun and the country was glorious. Some of the nurses had developed tuberculosis and one or two of them were patients. Their beds were pushed out into the air on sunny days. That must have been boring for them. They were hospitalised for months. That was the routine treatment at that time.

Some time later, I was assigned to Banstead. It was a very happy orthopedic convalescent center. I learned to make coffee in a huge urn at Banstead but not without some difficulty. After a few futile efforts that produced pale brown water, one of the nurses let me in on her secret. She told me to put gravy browning in it and it worked like a charm. I had my 21st birthday at Banstead. The patients wrapped me in a sheet and bounced me 21 times out on the lawn for all to see. During the night duty there, I was assigned to a room above the kitchen and I heard every dish cup and saucer go into the washer and come out again. That particular assignment was not long and that is all I remember of it.

We had a party for my 21st birthday at Banstead and Pauline managed to get the time off to come down for it. The 21st birthday was the official coming of age when as the saying goes you got the key of the door at home. That did not mean moving out to a place of one's own. It simply meant that one had a key to come in and out. I suspect that the rules of the house stayed the same. It was a significant birthday in those days.

I was transferred back to the London and that is where I made a fatal mistake. It was on night duty and again I simply could not sleep. I cannot tell you how terrible I felt. The more I tried to sleep the more awake I became. It really was torture. I began to be angry with my friends. Peg Crispin still remembers the day I went into her room when the bell went off to get up and threw back her covers angry because I had not slept all day. The day that Ghandi died in India (January 30, 1948) was the day that I was so desperate, I called home. My sister, Anne, answered the phone and I was crying. She called my father, who then called the Matron's office and I guess he did not mince his words. Consequently, I was reprimanded in the strongest tones for worrying my parents. I was weighed, examined, and ordered to report to the nurses' sick ward every morning for 15 or 30ccs of Chloral Hydrate. This is a medication for inducing sleep. I know this was given to me in a medicine glass that was not full. The dose had a minimal effect and I do not recall being asked if it was helpful or if I was sleeping any better. I was punished for these behaviors in I believe a totally unfair manner.

My London Hospital nursing certificate lists my behavior as fair. I never received a bad evaluation for my work. I was stunned at the time. To protest would have been useless, but it hurt me deeply. I am so thankful that I did not run home to my parents because my life would have been very different and I would have had to live with failure. My father wanted me to become an airline hostess. No disrespect to those who chose this career, but I would have been bored. Most of all I would have missed all the wonderful people who have touched my life. I need to physically keep moving so in that respect, nursing was made for me.

One of the difficulties of writing from memory is that stories come to me when I am away from the computer and, at the risk of confusing the reader, they are too special to me to leave out.

I worked a lot with patients suffering from cancer. I felt deeply for these individuals. Little did I know that in three years I would lose my father from this disease. I hardly knew him in my adult life and then he was gone.

On one particular ward for these patients, it was named Gurney, I had a significant task each night at midnight. In a small private room there was a very, very old London Hospital nurse. She had to have been from the Edwardian or even Victorian era. She was a great timekeeper. On the stroke of midnight her light would go on. Her request was simple enough; she asked for a cup of hot milk. Sounds easy enough, but wait. It had to be in a certain cup at the correct temperature, something like boiling. I got it right eventually and she went to sleep. Strange thing is, I never remember seeing her awake in the morning. She must have slept until breakfast time or longer. What a wasted opportunity! She must have had great stories. She was very superior in her manner and I was probably relieved to make the grade with her milk. So many of my memories are from night duty, no doubt because I was awake day and night. I believe that the London housed a thousand patients and most of them in the London itself. It was an incredible institution.

We received our weekly ration of sugar and margarine in small paper bags that we took back and forth to the dining room. What I cannot understand now is why I did not find a container for these, because the sugar bag invariably broke and the margarine got soft and melted. End of rations.

I worked in Fielden House and enjoyed it very much. This was the building for the private patients. There was a dumb waiter that carried good food. When sister had finished serving dinner, each floor would try to get the waiter and raided the treasures therein. Patients on soft diet were served delicious fish. It was sole cooked in milk. One day, Pauline got the catch of the day and as she was ready to pop it in her mouth sister returned. The ever-cool Pauline dropped it down the bib of her apron and there was a perfect outline of this little fish. We all did it because we were hungry. I was sneaking a cream cake out under my cloak on my way to tea and a lump of cream fell on the floor in front of me. This may sound silly, but we entertained one another with our tales of the near misses later in our rooms.

One of my duties that I remember was drawing Pentothal into a 30cc syringe in the presence of the anaesthesiologist Mr. Parry. In England he would be called the anaesthetist. He was a physician, but in UK the surgeons and anaesthetists were referred to as "Mr." This is in no way a derogatory form of address. Mr. Parry told me that the patient paid the highest compliment to the anaesthetist by allowing him to put the patient to sleep. Some surgeons would no doubt disagree with this. I never forgot this instruction.

While I was working in the private wards, Princess Elizabeth was married at Westminster Abbey. No TV, but someone had a radio on so that we could hear the service on a wireless in the ward. This was a major exception. The night before a group of us had rushed up to Buckingham Palace to see the Royal Family appear on the balcony. It was a mob of cheering, happy English people. We were near the fountain for those who have made the pilgrimage to the palace. The next afternoon, those of us who were off duty at 5pm dashed out again and I saw the carriage pass by. Actually, I only saw the feather in her hat, but I remember all the celebrations and it was so exciting.

I remember when a neurologist, Dr. Russell Brain (later Lord Brain), decided that the medical students on his service should learn to give enemas. The medical students did not enthusiastically welcome this. I had the challenge of teaching one of these bright men. He was neither happy nor proficient; in fact he was plain clumsy. Perhaps I should have used the line, "Don't you know what you are doing, Doctor," but I was not smart enough in those days and anyway the poor fellow had not a clue. Enemas did not come all prepackaged. That happened years later. We used soft soap and this had to melt and it was mixed with water. It was said that the students referred to Dr. Brain as "God." In the States, neurologists are in awe of his work and have described his book on neurology as the Bible. I recall that he was a very serious man. God was an apt description. We had classes from him and he was very bright but his subject never put me on fire.

Perhaps I should mention some of the equipment and duties that were state of the art. I never remember any patient having an intravenous infusion in the wards. We had to accompany our patients to and during surgery and return to the ward with them. No recovery rooms in those days. Medical students took the blood pressures, but the nurse removed the sutures and shortened the drains. I think I was quite skilled at that. It was my observation that I never wanted to have my gall bladder removed because so many of the patients died. This may not be factual; maybe I just ran into hard-luck surgeons. Patients did have a "thyroid crisis" and it was very frightening for them. This condition is also known as a thyroid storm. The symptoms are a sudden onset of fever, sweating, rapid heart rate and heart and lung problems. This can be fatal if untreated. One patient took off across the large hospital grounds. I am not sure now if I witnessed this or learned it by historical reference. I do remember struggling with patients and giving them Paraldehyde rectally as in an enema. This was to sedate them and calm their anxiety.

I believe that thyroid storm is very rare and with modern treatment probably does not happen anymore. I have no current information on this disease. As always, the best advice is check with your physician. Penicillin was new and handled like a narcotic. As students, we were told of the skills needed by nurses in the past in caring for example patients with pneumonia. It was really tough. We can only admire our nursing predecessors for their skills.

The twentieth century has seen dramatic changes in medicine and treatment. Given a choice, not many of us would want to go back to the so-called good old days. We live longer and therapies are expensive. This is the price of progress. During my own career, I have been a witness to so many of these changes. There were few diuretics and a diet of rice was often served but my memory may be a little off on the diet. I do know that patients at the London in severe heart failure often could not have a full cup of tea. I am sure of this fact and this is the reason.

I was on day duty and it was summer time. Pauline and I had dashed up to the West End during our three hours off. She knew a special place that served iced coffee that she enjoyed. I must have been a bystander. I was very excited because I was going home to Jersey the next day for my holiday. Well, I was on duty and my mind was not on duty. I gave a patient in severe heart failure a full cup of tea. Sister saw me and told me that I was irresponsible and asked me if I kept late nights. I wondered then and still do how I could have kept late nights because I was not off duty until 8:30pm and no one went out after that as far as I knew. Curfew time was 11pm following a day off. The patient, Mrs. C. witnessed this and she whispered to me that I was going to be a good nurse. I loved her for it, but there were other reasons for my fondness for her. She had intractable heart failure and her legs were filled with fluid. She was unable to move them. The fluid was removed through Southey's tubes. A Dr. Southey had devised this method. He was a Londoner, but in the past. Needles attached to drainage tubes were inserted in her legs and the fluid drained into a bucket. This supposedly relieved the tension and allowed the fluid to drain. The staphylococcus "bugs" in the ward must have had merry old time. However, sterile technique was sternly emphasized and I have no recollection that Mrs. C. was in danger from this point of view. This must have provided temporary relief but no doubt the fluid returned. I remember this lady and can see her now. She had a light complexion and wore glasses. I never saw her stand but she seemed to be a small person. Her heart was damaged but her smile was warm and kind. She never complained.

I preferred to care for patients with medical diseases. Many nurses did not, but we were a cross section of society with different backgrounds. When we had our first anatomy classes at Trueloves, I began to feel my preference. I took one look at the complicated base of the skull and knew that was not for me. The heart was infinitely more appealing. Four chambers I could understand. I was to become very involved with cardiac patients much later in my career at Bon Secours Hospital in Michigan in the United States.Life is a journey and the most long lived one is a small passage in time - I always say that I grew up at Bon Secours.

We sat for our final examination and all of my set passed. We mobbed the phones and I remember the telephone operator telling me, "What's your hurry, you all passed." He was trying to get through to Jersey. Some of the girls left immediately and some were invited to stay on for a fourth year. I had time to make up because of the time lost when I had rubella. Pauline also made up time for her chicken pox.

Pauline's dad came to pick us up in his Ford. We had many happy trips in that car on our days off in Kent. The car was piled high and we left together for new adventures, the first of which was a holiday in Austria.

I cannot leave the London without writing some thoughts and feelings. I am so proud of having been a student in that great old house. I wore my London hospital badge (pin) every day that I worked for almost fifty years. I gained more than I was able to give. When I entered those doors at the London in 1946, I had known that from a little girl, that was what I wanted. Something deep inside of me drew me to that profession like a magnet. Reaching the final post was never easy but I was never able to walk away from the London. Night duty was Hell but I managed to survive it. The patient nurse relationship is so engaging. It is an intimate relationship that I could not have found anywhere else. The joy of seeing someone returned to good health or the gentleness of being with someone at his or her death is not often appreciated in the world today. That is a great loss and no modern convenience can replace it. I would have given anything to be able to sleep on night duty. I am not sure that anything could have been done to help me.

Patients have no nationality they have needs. Listening is a pivotal requirement for all involved in health care. The listener becomes the key to the cure or the care. As students thrown in to this environment, permanent bonds are formed that are never broken. We learn from our mistakes, we are transformed in the process from the inept student to the confident practitioner and patient advocate. We survive through our stories that never become dull and are never out of date. Our reunions help us to remember our real selves. Nursing is a noble profession.

I have classmates who are close friends until this day. The patients gave me a special gift and that is that I am still able to see and in my imagination reach out and touch little O, enjoy a smile from Mrs. C. and another Mrs. C. at the Annex who had cancer of the esophagus and who never complained. So many more and gone so long ago. I made it and I am grateful.

CHAPTER FIVE

The Austrian Vacation – April 1949

Sometime before we left the London, Pauline and I decided to take a vacation on the Continent. As I write this in 1999, I find this to be very amusing. What, I wonder, did I use for money? Our pocket money was meager and must have only served its purpose to cover the bare necessities.

I do remember pressing our noses against the windows of all kinds of buildings for information. Pauline was the organizer and I was happy to follow her lead. She thinks that we really did this together. This is not as I remember it but it was a great adventure. Apparently no country was off limits. We looked at going to South Africa and India and many more that I cannot recall now. Switzerland was a favorite choice and we devoured the brochures and dreamed big dreams. Finally, Austria was chosen. The details escape me, but the price must have been right. Pauline was keen to go with the student hostel situation. This was economical and would have been good for me.

However, there were loud and determined protests from my family in Jersey. My father was adamant I was not going to be let loose in Europe moving from hostel to hostel and that was that! He must have paid for the holiday because we settled on a very nice hotel in Igls, a tiny village up in the mountains near Innsbruck. To reach it, we took a very small train that wound itself around the steep mountainside. Mr. O'Flaherty came up to the London in his trusty Ford car of uncertain age. We loaded our stuff and with a great deal of relief and excitement we said our farewells to our student days. The back of the car was piled high with my clothes etc! We went to Pauline's home and presumably packed once again for this big adventure. Pauline's parents were much less uptight about all this than mine. She had been evacuated to Wales for two years during the war so in a sense had left the nest at a much younger age.

We set off by train and took the boat to France. We then boarded a French train that, as I remember, was very different. We travelled all day and night, finally arriving at Basle in Switzerland in the early hours of the morning. As I write this, I am back on the platform remembering the sounds of the new day and thinking how clean and fresh everything seemed to be, like a fairyland.

I do not remember any meals on the journey, but I am guessing that we packed sandwiches and fruit or rather Mrs. O' Flaherty made sure that we had all that we needed. We boarded another train, which curled around the mountain into Austria.

I remember one very uncomfortable incident. At the border, a guard came in to check our passports. He was in uniform and spoke German. I stiffened involuntarily and for me it was a frightening moment, which threw me back into the Occupation days. The man was probably Austrian and I do not know if he spoke German or an Austrian dialect of sorts, but it was a sharp and sudden reminder of those difficult years not so long before.

In the afternoon we arrived in Innsbruck and soon were climbing the mountainside in the small train. Finally, we were in Igls. The hotel we stayed in was the Sport Hotel. In fact, it probably was the only hotel. We were shown to our room and at first we thought that they had forgotten to make the beds! Not true. What we saw was a feather duvet, which we used at night as bedcovers. In those days we referred to this as a feather bed. It was so cosy and I still like this form of bed covering to this day. Now that I live in Arizona and the Valley of the Sun, opportunities are rare in this climate for such a covering. But if the winter nights (all two or three of them!) are chilly, out comes the feather duvet.

There was also a bidet in the room, which we regarded with great curiosity, and no, we never used it! The hotel was small, but it had a marvellous chef. The food was especially appreciated after all the years of institutional cooking at the London. We were always hungry and the word diet had never affected our vanity or invaded our consciousness! Those were the days! We drank Apfelsaft, which was probably apple juice. It was delicious.

As I recall, we were the only young females in the hotel and we were soon joined by three young men. Such a deal! Also, Pauline had a pen pal named Walter, whose original nationality was Sudaten Deutsche. This country, originally part of Czechoslovakia (which no longer exists), was the first territory to be invaded and taken by Hitler and co. before the start of WWII. Walter at that time was a man without a country. I am not sure if he even had a passport. I do not know how Pauline found him as a pen pal, but I think that they had been corresponding for quite some time. Walter was a tall, blonde and handsome young man and he spoke English quite well. He had no money or means of transportation so he skied over to meet Pauline.

I remember a fifth man from Belgium joining the group. The other three were Englishmen. One of them was a teacher, another was a young naval lieutenant and, curiously, the third was a young Jewish man. I remember wondering why he would come to a country where his people had suffered so much? Perhaps he was on a secret mission. Sounds good, but I have no idea. This makes me think that young people tended to accept others with far less curiosity than later generations. It is probably a good thing. I remember a line in the song from the musical South Pacific, "You have to be taught, carefully taught, to hate the people your relatives hate."

Life in the village was simple and quiet. Pauline and I went on some interesting walks and when the ice was broken, the young men joined us. Nearby was a mountain named the Patschekoeffel. Skiing was obviously the sport of choice and families would pass the hotel on their way to the slopes. We took a cable car to the summit and it seemed that we were at the top of the world with all of that fresh pure air and blue, blue skies. It did not take many minutes for me to have the worst sunburn ever on my face. For several days I looked as though I had been in a prize fight! I could hardly open my eyes and the lids were so swollen.

We continued to amuse ourselves and I think that we must have been there for about a week. I did feel a strange sensation being surrounded by tall mountains, almost like being cut off from the world. It was not a comfortable feeling. We explored the ancient city of Innsbruck. We bought one or two souvenirs, one of which I have with me today. It is a small wooden plate with an engraving burned into the wood. It is in perfect condition and a wonderful reminder of a happy time. On it is engraved a hedgehog at the foot of a tree, which I believe has something to do with the name of the village.

It was time to leave and the young Belgian saw us off at the station on the Arlberg Express. The others had already gone on their way and to the rest of their lives, which I hope were good, productive, and healthy. We returned to Pauline's home and soon it was time for me to pack and return to Jersey. Pauline had chosen her new direction and decided to be a theater (operating room) nurse. I had not a clue of what I really wanted to do. I would have liked to join the Queen Alexandra Corps, the nursing division of the British army. It had a distinguished reputation and one traveled to foreign postings. That was appealing to me, the little girl who would not sleep one night away from home. I had come a long way! Fact is I was still too shy to do it. Now I know that I could have done it very well.

POSTSCRIPT FROM PAULINE:

"The money for the trip to Austria came from our parents. Our original idea was to hitchhike in France but when the Eldies heard of this they immediately said no and that they would pay for the holiday! Don't forget we were only getting 6-7 pounds a month then. The holiday could not have cost more than 25 pounds as that was the limit set by the post for foreign currency.

"I am sure that we both made the arrangements. Do you remember we had trouble with the passports as you were born in Jersey and I was born in Australia?"

Thank you, Pauline. I had forgotten about the hitchhiking!

CHAPTER SIX

Jersey Interlude
May – September 1949

Without a doubt, we only leave home once in a lifetime. The next time and the next forever on are visits. It took me a long time to realize this, but the truth is, having tasted the freedom of independence, there is no turning back. The transition is as painful for the parents as it is for the child.

I had returned to Jersey and the Island was as beautiful as ever. Probably even more so having lived in a city for four years. My parents were the same but I was not! My father was sure that I was back home safe and sound. My mother had not changed her expectations of me and I was still the eldest, but a child. It was a painful period of adjustment.

Part of my problem was that I had not chosen which career path to pursue. There were several options available to me. At that time, the nursing education system meant that additional study was recommended. The primary and most popular choice was midwifery and really it was almost a mandatory requirement. The others were the care of sick children, infectious diseases and the mentally ill. There were hospitals that specialized in these areas. I had been introduced to all of these diagnoses at the London but further study was available.

I remember caring for a patient with typhoid fever at the London. He was a sailor and he was in a regular ward, screened off, and his care was isolated from the other patients. There was no spread of the disease and I never encountered any other patient with typhoid fever. I remember this patient very clearly. We also had many patients with venereal disease in the active phase of their illness. Scarlet fever, diphtheria, and polio were still prevalent, as I recall, and these patients would not have been cared for in a general hospital.

The care of the mentally ill was even less attractive. I had witnessed electric shock therapy at the London and I thought it was all rather frightening. I enjoyed the pediatric experience and would have liked to do this at the distinguished Great Ormond Street Hospital for Sick Children. The hospital was in London and it no doubt had many candidates waiting for acceptance. So it was midwifery that was the best and most appealing option. I looked at several hospitals. The Radcliffe in Oxford and a hospital in Edinburgh, Scotland but finally applied to St.Helier Hospital in Carshalton in Surrey.

By an unusual coincidence I was born in the parish of St.Helier in Jersey. St.Helier was a hermit who, it is reported, lived on a rock in Jersey in the year 543. The rock still exists and is part of Elizabeth Castle. This castle, with a unique history of its own, is only accessible when the tide is out. It is really a fun and historic landmark. It can be enjoyed today by walking out to the Castle when the tide is out but one must be mindful that the tide also comes in and of the dangers if one delays too long.

St.Helier Hospital was in the county of Surrey and I had really enjoyed living there during the Banstead experience. It was just near and yet far away from London. It was suburbia at its best.

The letters of application and acceptance all took time but, to the relief of all, I was accepted. Until I returned to England, I continued to live at home. I was 22 and a very successful freeloader but that never crossed my mind and my parents never mentioned it to me. I wonder what they thought. When I returned from Surrey following my midwifery course, I overheard my father telling a friend that I had actually paid my airfare back to the Island. I was shocked and hurt at the time. I never forgot it and I never made that mistake again. It was not until I went to the London that I had handled money and there was little of that as a student nurse. There was little money in the Occupation; my parents spent every penny (reischmark) on food. There was no expectation of having a job as a teenager in those times. As far as I know, that was an American custom. I think that work experience would have been of enormous help to me.

THE PUPIL MIDWIFE
SEPTEMBER 1949 - FEBRUARY 1950

I arrived at the hospital on a Sunday, having flown over from Jersey that morning. Soon after I arrived, I met another girl named Ida Watson. So began a friendship that continues until this day. Ida was from Yorkshire, a large county in the north of England. She had a very different accent.

Pauline, my friend from the London, was from Kent, a county in the southeast of England. Both of these families took me in and made me one of their own. My memory bank is filled with gems of kindness from these two families. Pauline's father was a naval man and a lover of classical music. He and Pauline had great discussions and he often had a new recording waiting for her when we arrived for our day off. I was woefully ignorant and some of it I enjoyed and some I endured. The important part was that I was learning and feeling my way in a new world.

I have many memories of Mrs. O'Flaherty, and I can still taste the marvellous meals that she prepared for us and all of this with rationing still in place. She brought us our breakfasts in bed and we fell back to sleep for another couple of hours. It is important to note that we were working a 48-hour week. This was described as revolutionary at the time. We were both dead tired and most amazingly I did not have to get up to go the bathroom at night in those days!

She fed us supper, breakfast, dinner, and tea all in 24 hours. She truly was a wonder. My favorite memory is of her doing dishes at her kitchen sink. She was a petite little lady and she wore what seemed to be rubber gloves that were many sizes too large for her. Pauline and I equipped with two tea towels, did the drying part of the operation. We solved the problems of the world and we had great conversations, combined with a lot of laughter. I can see her now

Sheila at St. Brelade's Bay, Jersey 1950.

A group of Jersey General Hospital nurses in August 1950. Sheila is second on the right.

Sheila (aged 21) with sister Anne (aged 14) and "Paddy" in 1948.

pushing her glasses back in place on her nose with her finger in a glove that looked enormous. Such memories are priceless.

The Watsons were the best that Yorkshire had to offer. A farming family of comfortable means they lived in a huge house named Ellercourt. Ida also had a younger sister named Mary who was a real character. The Watson girls had been sent to boarding school during the war because German POWs were billeted on the farm. Very different from my experience with the German forces as the Occupying power. More about this family later in my story.

The pupil midwife experience was very different. I was now a qualified nurse and with that came new responsibilities. I remember how odd it felt to give a narcotic without supervision. I checked the dose many times before administering it. I was with nurses from all over the UK with diverse educational experiences. There were three of us from the London and one of the Sister tutors was a Londoner. We always referred to the hospital as LH. Now it is known as the Royal London Hospital.

The change of environment, or perhaps my new status as a Registered Nurse, provided me with a new sense of freedom. We were allowed to bring one another breakfast to our rooms on our day off duty. This was a real treat. We were living in the nurses' residence, dormitory style, and that meant that at least for one day we did not have to get up and go to the cafeteria. Sounds simple but it meant a lot. I had my share of night duty but it was of shorter duration. I missed the class day system at the London, which had apparently been copied from the American model. At St.Helier, we had to get up for classes when we were on night duty and I found this to be brutal.

We were rotated to all of the departments. Paul and Linda were the names in vogue at that time. There must be lots of 49 year olds with those names in England. The mothers remained in bed for five days. Breast-feeding was the norm. At dinner time each day they were served with a pint of Guinness. I was thankful that this tradition did not extend to the nurses' dining room. Now I am wondering if this was for their nourishment or to flavor the breast milk. I do not recall any tipsy babies.

Our experience was thorough and after the postpartum wards it became more specialized. We rotated through the antenatal clinic and I enjoyed this very much. We learned to do a physical examination of the patient and to palpate the abdomen to assess the position of the fetus. This was important during the delivery process. Blood pressure was monitored and we learned about and cared for patients with toxemia. This is a serious complication of pregnancy. I have no knowledge of the present management of this complication now.

The nursery was a delight and we were taught to carry two babies out to the mothers at one time. We did this with ease. It sounds horrifying now; I would have trouble with one. I do not recall any sick babies but preemies were plentiful. No incubators, no monitors, no neonatal units. Just us and God in those days.

The preemie nursery consisted of a series of private rooms. They ranged from stifling hot to normal in temperature. I recall one tiny little boy. He could have fitted into a man's hand with room to spare. The babies were fed every half-hour, day and night. My experience in this unit was when I was on night duty. It had one big advantage: there was no time to think about sleep.

I was assigned to the room with the tiny boy. The room was like an oven and we were fully gowned and gloved. This little baby lay in a regular crib (cot). The caliber of the feeding tube was truly minute. I was sure that I would hurt him and as often as I could I had Ida help me.

As one moved through the rooms with each half-hour, the babies were bigger. At a certain stage they begin to look like little old people. They even showed personality traits. I loved them. They would curl their tiny fingers around mine and they were precious.

Writing this story for readers in England, Jersey, and the United States seems like a good time to mention something that I have discovered in this process. When I began this adventure I believed that Americans and the English people spoke a common language. I was wrong and I must admit that until this project I never gave this fact a second thought. What I am going to write next is a clear example. There are words that have the same meaning but transmit a totally different frame of reference.

For example, a routine responsibility at the end of each shift involved boiling the *teats* from the baby bottles. In the US they are *nipples*. Woe to the student that let the teats boil dry. The odor was noxious and it hung around for hours. The ward sister had an acute sense of smell.

It was inevitable the day arrived when I was to admit my first patient. The admitting room was on the ground floor. The patients were assessed and prepared for transfer to the delivery room. There was a bell to summon a midwife in an emergency situation. I walked into the room and greeted a young woman in her late twenties, in active labor. I began the admission process. I was carefully reading the instructions on the wall when the patient yelled, "Nurse, the baby is coming and I lost my first one at (she named a district in London)"

There are no words in any language at any time that can describe the terror that I felt at that moment. I have never been strong at lifting but I had that patient on the table in a snap! She was fully dressed complete with corsets, stockings (hose) hooked to her garters (suspenders). By the time the midwife arrived I had a slippery baby in my hands. Best of all, we were all alive.

I went on to deliver my quota of ten or twelve babies but under controlled conditions in the delivery room. The first of these bouncing babies was a girl, and, yes, I remember both of her names; the first one was Sheila. I knew at the end of this rotation that my hands were too small and my fingers too short for doing pelvic examinations.

Ida invited me to her home in Yorkshire and we were to sit for the final examination in Leeds. This city was the northerly location where the examination was held and not too far from the Watson home. I had never been north before so I eagerly looked forward to this opportunity. There were two sections to the midwifery course. One was to complete the first six months and receive the CMB (Certification of the Central Midwives Board). Many of the students, and Ida was one, elected to complete the next six months and become an SCM (State Certified Midwife).

To complete the second part the student went out into the community (usually not in the best environment) into the patients' homes. The patient was followed through the antenatal period, delivery and through the postpartum phase. This was accomplished on foot or on a bike. The student was responsible for the complete and total care of the mother and infant day and night. The responsibility was monitored by the instructor midwife. At the successful completion of this second phase the student received the SCM. The same guidelines were in place. A physician must be called for complications. The qualified nurse became an independent practitioner.

This career track was not for me. I was certain that I did not want to spend my life saying, "Push, mother, push" but it did answer some questions. I knew that I enjoyed most of all caring for patients with medical diseases.

The six months went by and we set off for Yorkshire by train. I really enjoy this form of transport. I realize that those that commute each day may find this to be an outlandish statement. There is something very pleasant seeing the landscape   roll by.

We arrived in Yorkshire and made our way to Ellercourt. What a joyful family. Everyone was bustling around because Mr. and Mrs. Watson were about to celebrate their 25th wedding anniversary. Ida and I became a part of the preparations. There were pastries to pick up and all manner of things to do floral arrangements, etc. Guests were arriving, trains needed to be met and it was a busy time. I thought that 25 years was a very long time to be married and that they must be very old.

Ida knows and loves Yorkshire better than any tour guide. She had grown up in a farming community that was both warm and close. The social life for the young folk was exciting and there seemed to be one continuous round of balls. Ida had a driver's license and use of the family car. Our generation was no different from any other; wheels equalled freedom.

We travelled all over and spent wonderful days in the ancient city of York. This all took much longer than today; there were no motorways. Speed and convenience deprive one of the beauties of the countryside. The architecture of the north was very different from the south. Lots of red brick and what appeared more sturdy buildings. This was my perception at the time.

During all these years there have been many visits to both Yorkshire and Kent, I never had an encounter with either of these wonderful families that was not warm and welcoming. A word about Mary Watson, Ida's younger sister. She was full of life and always up on the latest doings of the young folks, of the farming community romances, engagements and future weddings. Mrs. Watson had a turkey business of sorts. She raised turkeys for Christmas. Mary's responsibility was to collect the eggs. Unfortunately Mary tended to be clumsy or perhaps she was distracted but she spent a lot of time begging us to ask for eggs. Fair to say Mary made a definite crack in the profits. (Sorry about that, Mary, I found it to be irresistible!)

We took our midwifery examinations in Leeds, a big city in the center of Yorkshire, and later we both received positive results. The examination was held in a hospital. I clearly remember walking down one of the corridors and thinking how different it was from the London. It was a perfectly fine hospital, but it was not the London. That great institution had a lasting effect on me. After the examination, we went shopping and Mrs. Watson, who must have accompanied us, bought a purse of Ostrich skin. Crazy memories as clear to me as if it were yesterday.

I returned to Jersey. I paid for my fare! Ida went on to complete part two of the midwifery course and Pauline was gaining experience as a theater nurse.

THE GENERAL HOSPITAL - JERSEY
MAY 1950 - NOVEMBER 1952

I applied for a staff nurse position at the General hospital that was the only hospital in the Island. It had a history of having been an

103

Pupil midwives 1950. Left to right: Lorna (Davies) Timmins, Sheila Le Sueur.

Mother and Father on the occasion of their Silver Wedding, August 31st 1950.

Jersey General Hospital Battle of Flowers Float, in 1951. Sheila on the right.

institution for the down and out before the war but the post war progress had changed all that.

The alternatives to the hospitals were known as nursing homes. These institutions were under private ownership and they operated on a fee-for-service basis. The medical needs of the community were maintained by private general practitioners. They billed the patient. Health insurance was a concept not even in the imagination.

I am working from memory but as I recall anesthesia was given by general practitioners that obviously must have had specialized training. The physicians quite naturally had their preferences as to choice, but I believe the patient also had a choice, not only in physician, but of hospital and/or nursing home. There were two or three general surgeons who were well respected by the community.

When I arrived back in the Island, my mother was in Bon Air Nursing Home recovering from a hysterectomy. One evening driving home after visiting my mother, my father told me that he had not been feeling well. He had taken some powder and he felt better. I did not pursue this but I do wonder if this "powder" was medication that he took for gout.

My sister just reminded me that this powder was from his brother, who used it for stomach ailments for wounds he suffered in WWI. One day, we mistook it for icing sugar, and iced a cake with it. It was awful. Note to readers: Do not use stomach powder as cake icing.

My father was never a drinker but I do remember several attacks of gout during the Occupation. During those years there were no medicines. He used to put a piece of brown paper on his foot and my mother would literally iron the painful area. This did produce some relief. This was an old remedy: 150 years earlier English soldiers used brown paper and hot wax for the same result. My mother came home after her surgery, and as per the norm, had a protracted convalescence.

The Island is only 45 square miles and before the war the population was approximately 50,000. The health care system was different from England but it certainly seemed to meet the needs of the population - certainly I do not remember dissatisfaction with the system. During the war, the hospital was occupied by the Germans. Wards were set-aside for the civilian population. Dr. John Lewis in his book, "A Doctor's Occupation," memorializes the work and the professionalism of the nurses who worked under incredibly difficult circumstances. Of one fact I am certain, those nurses were second to none. Their work and dedication belongs to the history of the Island and to the nursing profession.

I settled in and there were more new friends and a very happy period had begun. The hospital had an atmosphere of progress and optimism. I started work on the male surgical ward and I was very happy to be close to home and back in the Island. My Father could not have been happier.

The Island was beautiful. It was early summer and the beaches were a paradise. Work consumed a great deal of time and I do not remember the length of the workweek. It was easy to drop in at home for a couple of hours and every other Sunday I had the whole day off after 1pm. It seemed like a miracle. The work was challenging but not impossible. I enjoyed working with the student nurses. I also felt good about caring for my fellow Islanders.

What I realized many years later that I have always been happier in a smaller and more intimate environment. Sooner or later it had to happen and I was once more on night duty. This was no easier for me. I had a horrendous time trying to sleep. Sometimes I would get up and go home. The work itself had never been a problem for me. In fact, in many ways it was easier. We still only had two shifts, day and night duty.

I pretty much rotated to all of the adult wards. I also spent a lot of time in the paediatric ward on both day and the night shift. I remember one or two young children and had the immense pleasure of reading their wedding announcements in the Jersey Weekly paper many years later. Both were little boys. One infant had a feeding problem and there was often more food on my uniform than in his mouth. The other (I think he was a redhead) had severe burns all over both hands. I had to debride (peel) the skin on his fingers down to his nail beds. He was such a good little boy and each day I dreaded doing his dressing more than the day before.

Recently one of the baby's mother's death notice was in the Jersey Weekly Post and I was happy to see that the little baby, now a grown man, still thrives. Over the years I have remembered so many patients. They all had a subtle influence on my work and my life.

I believe I should mention the protocol for children who were admitted for T and A's - tonsils and adenoids. They were in a separate ward and hospitalized for about four days. The parents did not see them from admission until discharge. I do not remember visiting hours for the other children, but it was usually one or two days each week. This was normal in those days. The nurses spent a lot of time with the children. That was the way the world worked. Now I think that this regulation, or whatever one would call it, was brutal.

Friends from childhood were in the Island and we were able to play tennis. I was not competitive but the courts were right next to our home and it was just very pleasant. My father was spending a lot of time on the golf course. He had a great tan and was losing weight, which we thought was from the exercise. Little did we realize that this tanned and slimmer body disguised a growing and inoperable tumor.

One night duty memory comes back to me now. One rather cold night the sister in charge sent me out in the ambulance to one of the hotels. A visitor had hung himself in a hotel at La Colette. I was to ride in the ambulance and retrieve the body. The ambulance driver and I set off and we talked a little. I was trying to imagine this awful scene and my role in it. We left the hospital and drove past the harbor along the coast over Mt. Bingham. The tide was in and the sea air was cold and damp. I was shivering in my cotton uniform, trying not to convey my fear to the ambulance driver. I tried to imagine the task before me and what I needed to do when we arrived. All too soon the ambulance came to a screeching halt and we were outside the hotel. The police met us and, bless them; they were already at the scene. The man was dead and they had retrieved and taken custody of the body. I never saw the victim but I was, luckily, off the hook! We returned to the hospital and, to be honest, I was filled with relief. I never had another assignment like that again.

The opportunities for off-duty activities living in an island were infinitely more attractive to me than those in a huge city like London. In the summer, there were picnics on the beach. I was working with a young group of nurses and we were a small but cohesive staff.

My parents were to celebrate their silver wedding August 1950. A reception was held at the house and a dinner followed that evening at the Bay View Hotel. Everything went off as planned. One small snag: I arrived promptly at the house for the afternoon reception with a bunch of hungry nurses. They proceeded to eat everything in sight. There followed a lot of activity in the kitchen to replenish the sandwiches and the pastries. My mother who had zero culinary skills as a bride had spent the following 25 years reaching perfection She was an excellent pastry cook. My father always took pride in the fact that we maintained a good table. It was a happy day and the expectations were that this most happy union would continue.

My father must have had a recurrence of not feeling well. He had made the acquaintance of Doctor Maitland who came to the Island after the war. He consulted him on a professional basis. I am not certain if I knew this at that time. Dr. Maitland was one of the physicians who served as an anesthesiologist at the hospital.

All too soon I learned the truth. A chest x-ray revealed a tumor of the trachea that was wrapped around the aorta. This accounted for the angina-like symptoms that my father was experiencing. Dr. Maitland told me that the tumor was almost certainly malignant but because my father was such a special person, he would be sent to England for exploratory surgery. He told me that I was not to tell my parents. I was devastated. One thinks one's parents will go on forever.

I knew he had a chronic cough and he had a childhood history of pulmonary problems. I also realized that he was a long-time smoker. Still the news was tough. My father always had a fear of death because his father had died of cancer of the trachea in his 40s.

He also was a smoker. He was only nine years old when his father died and life became much more difficult for the Le Sueur family.

I did not know where to turn, but I found myself in the Nursing office in front of the Matron (Nursing director). I blurted out that my father had cancer. She said "Nurse, your cap is crooked" and I was dismissed. My despair turned to anger at her. Maybe that was her technique. I had no one to talk to. Fearful was I that the secret would be discovered. The next day I was expected at home. I remember loitering in the town wishing the ground would swallow me up and that I would not have to face my parents. Somehow I got through the visit. They were still waiting for the results of the x-ray.

On the following Sunday, my father picked me up in the car at the hospital. He was wearing his slippers and he was close to tears. He told me that he was going to St. Mary's Hospital in Paddington, London. He had immense confidence in Dr. Maitland and so the plans were made. He was operated on and it was an open-and-shut case. My mother called that evening and she now knew the truth; the tumor was malignant. The instructions were that my father should not be told because, and I quote, "it would kill him!" I cannot believe that I ever accepted such stupid logic but that was common practice at the time. I was a daughter and not a nurse in that situation.

My sister, who was seventeen then, had a close and special relationship with her father and she was to remain in ignorance for fear that she would slip and tell him the diagnosis.

I was called to Matron's office one morning. She was now public enemy No.1 in my opinion. She informed me that I was to accompany a patient suffering from a brain tumor to England for surgery. Clearly she was giving me an opportunity to visit my father

Tennis in Jersey. Sheila (right) with Margaret Grimshaw.

Ida (Watson) Timms with 'Peter'' at Corbiere Lighthouse, 1950.

Pam (Millard) Carver 1957.

in hospital in London. She was a much wiser lady than I gave her credit for being. I never forgot this act of kindness. The plane was a small seven seater. The seats were removed and the patient was on a stretcher on the cabin floor. So the three of us set off the pilot, the patient, and me. The journey lasted about an hour and mercifully the patient appeared to be comfortable. He was almost in a coma and could not communicate to me. I never learned the end or beginning of his story.

My father was surprised but not alarmed to see me. My mother wore emotional armor to protect him and I adapted to the secret. He returned to the Island having been told that the tumor was very large but all would be well. From the day they returned to our home, my mother never left the house until he died eight and one-half months later. She was the primary caregiver and she guarded the actual diagnosis from all except my father's sister and their closest friends. She shopped by phone.

So began the lies in a family that never lied to anyone. The advice was very wrong but it was accepted at that time as common practice. I can still feel the horror of those lies. My father received all that was possible from a physical point of view, but emotionally he was isolated and alone. He believed that the tumor was gone and that he would recover. We were powerless to help him. This was accepted. His physician gave him excellent care. The prognosis was that he would live more than six months and less than nine. He lived for eight and a half months.

My mother cared for him lovingly and tirelessly. My sister, Anne, only learned the diagnosis from my mother a few days before our father died. The truth would have been much easier for her from the beginning. Mother told her at lunchtime, warning her not to cry because he might hear her, and with that sent her back to work.

Anne was an apprentice in dressmaking at the time. She, not surprisingly, burnt some material with the iron and was rebuked for that. She told her boss that her father was dying and was told to pull herself together and get on with her work. So much for the stiff upper lip! I came home each day and gave him a bed bath. He had clean linen sheets every day. These had been embroidered by my mother as part of her trousseau.

The hardest part for my father was that he could not eat. Food was no sooner down than it was up. Friends brought him delicacies but nothing worked and he steadily lost weight. He got up and dressed each day and before he died I could almost carry him up the stairs to his bedroom. Dr. Maitland made an extra visit each evening at bedtime and gave him a morphine injection. I do mean every evening for eight and one-half months. Everyone liked my Father and his doctor was no exception. He had a solution of oral morphine, which he took during the day. His pain was well managed.

During WW1 my father had served in the Royal Naval Air Service. He was always proud of having been in this new branch of the armed services. Like all Channel Islanders he had volunteered to do his bit. During that time he met Bill Sykes (whose real name was Arnold) and a friendship was begun that was to last a lifetime. Uncle Bill, as we called him, came to live with us for some time and he helped care for his old friend. Friends are priceless and we all loved him.

My father was not an educated man. With the death of his father, the family fortunes were all but lost, based on the fact my grandmother made bad business decisions. She was a homemaker, a mother of those times. So he did not have a private school education that his brother and sister had.

My father went to work at a very young age to help his mother and sister. He had a sharp mechanical mind and could work magic with any engine. During the Occupation, these talents served him well. He made a machine that crushed potatoes into flour. This flour was quite tasty and enabled our mother to create many a meal. Later he built a threshing machine, which he somehow secretly transported to his farmer friends and that gave us all flour. If he had been discovered, the penalty would have been severe and swift, particularly when the Germans were suffering from lack of rations.

He was rough of tongue but a gentleman, decent in all his dealings, protective of his family and a devoted husband. He died

May 19, 1951, in the mid-morning. I was on night duty. The home sister woke me up and told me the news. I went home to a broken-hearted mother and a frightened sister.

A friend from the hospital helped me to "lay him out," as was the custom. My mother told me that, before he died, he walked to the bathroom, got back into the bed and told her that he felt awful. They held each other in their arms. Both were crying and with that he died.

Women did not attend funerals at that time. We made all the arrangements. My sister and I insisted on going to the funeral. I knew that I could not let him go alone. Some of the men at the funeral were uncomfortable with our presence. We sat in the car and did not go to the gravesite. Our mother remained at home with our Aunt Rita. She was his elder and only sister and had mothered him as a child during his many pulmonary illnesses. The floral tributes were so many that it required two hearses. The service was at a Methodist church and burial was at Almorah Cemetery. Our mother's first visit out of the house since she brought him home from the hospital was to the cemetery. She hired a taxi. She was broken hearted and she was 51 years old.

GRIEF, ANGER, AND SELFISHNESS

Our mother somehow continued to exist. She was very, very angry with everyone and it was often embarrassing. In a year, she had celebrated her silver wedding and no sooner that was over she watched her husband die. Anne took the brunt of it and for years it affected their relationship.

Mother was a very strong woman and eventually did get on with her life. She was offered jobs but refused them. Clearly she had to do something. Financially they had been struggling to get back on their feet after the Occupation years. They had everything going for them.

I returned to the hospital, and Anne to learning dressmaking. I made plans to go on holiday to France and off I went. Now I cannot believe that I did this. I went with one of the nurses at the hospital and had a good time. Where, I wonder, was my grief? I have no idea how Anne felt. So that is why I wrote selfishness at the top of this chapter. I must admit that it was something of a relief after the stress of the last year, but I am certain that I was not conscious of this fact.

The day I was due to return home I went directly to the hospital. My mother had gone to meet me and of course I was not there. She was so angry that I shall never forget it. She was losing control of everything in her life. Eventually the hard feelings dissolved and life went on. I continued to work at the hospital.

Mother decided to take in visitors (tourists) during the summer season. She served breakfast and dinner and she worked so hard. She fed them very well. She was so tired that she would fall asleep at night at the kitchen table. Home as we knew it was gone forever. Strangers had invaded our space and none of us enjoyed it. We always had a nice home. It was well furnished and it was squeaky clean. I lived at the hospital but Anne and my mother lived in one room. Both Anne and I hated this time but I do not recall that either of us felt resentment. We helped as much as we were able. This continued for two summers and in the winter there were lodgers. One tried to shave in our dining room and Mother threw him out.

In 1952, I was restless and I must have seen no future in being a staff nurse at the hospital. Some of my friends were also moving on. I had it in my head that I needed to travel abroad and I hunted for opportunities in the nursing journals. There were several advertisements for British educated nurses. I decided that Rhodesia in Africa sounded like a possibility. My mother never objected, but when I found an ad for Detroit, Michigan, in the US, she encouraged me in that direction. Her family had emigrated to Detroit years before and both of her parents had died there. Still living were two sisters and a brother and their families. My mother was married by the time her parents left the Island in 1926.

The advertisement was quite unusual and it had a lot of red flags. They would pay for the fare to the US and they wrote to me that all American nurses married doctors. I remember reading the letter to the other nurses and how we all laughed at that. My aunt went to investigate this place and it was a horror. She was locked in a room and the lady who presented herself was one tough woman. It was an alcoholic rehabilitation place and looked very unusual. Actually, it looked like a dump. My aunt wondered if she would get home in one piece! She wrote by the next mail to come out independently and then look for work. That is how the decision and the plans were made. I intended to come for 15 months and then return to Jersey.

Was it fate? Destiny? I shall never know. In life we all make important decisions when we hardly know the world. Education, career, marriage. There seems to be such urgency. We are ageless and health and death are never on the list. I was about to take an enormous step into a new country once more, to a different culture and to meet a family I only knew from photographs. I thought that at least they spoke English. Well, I cannot say that now!

POSTSCRIPT:

There are surprises in this adventure. Anne reads all that I write and it is enormously helpful. She tells me that in fact our father was very proud that I was a nurse and that he would tell all of their friends that his daughter was at the London Hospital learning to be a nurse. I never knew that. There are tears in my eyes as I write this.

Professor Sommerness has already edited the manuscript, but I must add these words "This book is my gift to you, Dad, along with the grandchildren that you never met."

CHAPTER SEVEN

Travel Plans And The Journey To The United States

I remember very little about the actual preparations for the journey. Some of the other nurses at the hospital were making similar career moves and we were all caught up in a general air of excitement. I am wondering now why was I in such a rush. Why could I not have waited until spring or summer? Time moves more slowly when one is young and I seem to remember that I felt an urge to get on with my career. This trip was not to be a permanent move for me. I planned to spend no more than 15 months in America and I never ever intended to leave Jersey on a permanent basis.

Pauline later asked me why I moved so far away and why I had not considered returning to England. Truth is, I have no idea. I had it in my head that British nurses traveled abroad but only within the British Empire, because the rest of the world was not part of my world. I knew that I wanted to travel. The real question was just where would it be. It was only later that America became a possibility and my mother reminded me that her family lived in Detroit, Michigan. It is important to mention that travel to America had been very much out of reach to the ordinary person.

In life we make major decisions when we barely understand the game of life itself. Perhaps I was running from or toward something. I really do not have the answer. Marriage was the expectation for a young woman in those days. Imagine making such a decision that would last a lifetime with one person. I was far too immature and shy to have done that.

I do remember going to the American Embassy in London to apply for a visa. There was a quota system for entry into the United States in place at that time. The British quota, unlike those for the other European countries, was never full. This was probably because the currency restrictions at that time made it impossible. My British passport lists that my allowance was limited to fifty pounds sterling. That was all that I was allowed to take out of the country.

I remember walking from the Bond Street underground station into Grosvenor Square on a beautiful sunny day and seeing the American Embassy. It was, as I see it now in my memory, a white Victorian mansion, gracious and appealing. The square was filled with tall and leafy trees. I seem to remember walking up the steps into a foyer and being directed to a room on my right. It had a warm and welcoming feeling.

Anne and I stayed at the Marriott Hotel in Grosvenor Square in 1995 before we went to Jersey to celebrate our 50 years of Liberation. I found no trace of this beautiful memory. The Embassy was in the same location but that was all. What I saw was a huge concrete building which felt to me to be cold and forbidding and was no doubt built to withstand any assault which may be directed against it. I wanted to go inside, but I hesitated, looked at the guard and walked away. Times change and needs change. I am sure that the old house became too small, less efficient, and very vulnerable. WWII with all of its horror and destruction had only been over for less than ten years, but that did not alter the fact that my first walk around Grosvenor Square was in far more innocent times.

I believe that I was given a physical examination or that I had to take proof of one. I especially recall being interviewed by the American Vice Consul. In my passport, he signed his name as being a Mr. Francis J Heflin and he was the Vice Consul in London, England. All that I remember about my conversation with him was that he was friendly and he told me that Detroit was a very cold place where they played ice hockey. Perhaps he was a Southerner or from California? I was not attuned to the differences in the American accent at that time. I found that Detroit was not only cold in the winter but unbearably hot in the summer.

My immigration visa number was #13452 and I entered the United States at the port of New York, November 26, 1952. The visa process must have taken several months because I know that I went to the Embassy on a lovely English summer day. Perhaps it was only legal for a limited time and I therefore had no choice of date of departure. Somewhere along the line I believe that my fingerprints were taken and I have often wondered if they are in the files of the FBI!

I know I was questioned several times and asked if I had ever been associated with any Nazi groups. I explained my life during the five years of Nazi occupation and they were more than satisfied that I was no threat to the United States of America. Dennis Ryan (my Father had worked for the Cleveland Garages which was owned by the Ryan family) gave me his old trunk that he had used at university in England. Dennis was very fond of my parents. He was so kind and attentive to my father during his illness. In a sense, they had a father-son relationship. My mother was able to repay this kindness by helping Dennis take care of his young family during a very difficult time in his life some months later.

The trunk was more than adequate and my initials were painted on it. I had it for many years until it finally gave out. I never used it for travel after I arrived in the United States, but it did great service for storage. Actually it was quite attractive with my Cunard Liner labels on it. The only things that I remembered packing were my records. They were the old 78s and all of them were of the American musicals that I had seen on the London stage. They must have weighed a ton! It makes no sense to me now to take them for so short a time. They must have meant a great deal to me.

I was very lucky to have a school friend whose father was a Captain on the Cunard line. He was on the New Zealand run, but he kindly arranged for me to have special attention and a nice cabin on the Queen Elizabeth for my journey to America. There were flowers and a huge bowl of fruit waiting for me in the cabin. My cabin mates were duly impressed.

I do not remember leaving the General Hospital in Jersey, but Miss Piper, the Matron, graciously provided me the necessary references for me to apply for licensure in the United States. This, as I recall, was a break from normal procedure. I have them to this day.

Anne was 18 and I was 25. I have absolutely no memory of saying good-bye to her. The difference in our ages had always been significant and as a small child she broke so many of my toys, I regarded her as bit of a terror. I had a dollhouse and as a toddler she discovered how to get in it and I was very upset. It was furnished with miniatures which she managed to destroy. I was sick and tired of hearing, "She is only a baby." We often laugh about all this now.

Back to the packing. This has never been my forte, so I imagine my mother did most of it. Before I was to leave for America, I had an invitation to a major event in England. It was Mary Watson's 21st birthday celebration and it was a formal affair. I was not going to miss that! I have already written of the hospitality of the Yorkshire farming community and this was no exception. As much preparation went into this event as in any wedding. Mary worked for months on the plans. The 21st birthday was the coming of age for all of us and supposedly one was given the key to the door at this time. Actually, it marked the separation from childhood to adulthood.

Mary Watson's 21st. truly was a gala affair. It was a wonderful party and after a week with the family, I left Yorkshire for a journey that was to change my life. The trunk and I headed for Southampton to board the *Queen Elizabeth.*

I mentioned my difficulty with packing a suitcase. I remember telling Ida when we were taking a train for London on one of our holidays not to worry because someone always helped me carry my suitcase. It seems that I frequently pack too much. Well, on this occasion we were struggling through the London underground when my suitcase popped open. No one came to my aid and Ida was given no option but to help me. She soon found out that someone indeed does help me and this time it was her! Through the years we have had many a laugh over this. To this day, I have help with my luggage when I travel.

As matter of fact, I have recently returned from Washington DC. I simply cannot reach the overhead bin in an airplane. I was struggling to put my carry-on suitcase in the bin without any chance of success when two men came to my aid. They were also trying to clear the aisle for the other passengers to board the plane. On the return journey, I realized I better not press my luck and I checked both of my bags.

My mother came over from Jersey, or perhaps she had been at Mary's party, but I do remember her coming to see me on to the *Queen Elizabeth* and we said our good-byes. She had been a widow for less than two years and I think she was pleased that her family would finally be meeting one of her children.

A few people had told me little things about Americans, but I knew very little of what to expect. The social worker at the hospital told me two things: Americans ate their beetroot (beets) warm in a kind of syrup and that they had colored bathroom towels, unlike the white ones in England. I was also warned that I would be chewing gum and that I would meet and marry someone named Elmer. I never did take to chewing gum and Elmer never materialized. I did care for a patient once named Elmer and I told him and his wife my story.

Ida had told me about and had shown me some of the old American airfields in England. Many of the buildings were empty and they were overgrown with weeds and had fallen into disrepair. Years later, from movies and documentaries I saw, they came to life for me. When I first arrived in London in 1945, there were American servicemen walking around and they looked very glamorous. That was our perception because they were Americans.

After the war I saw pictures for the first time of cousins I had only been hearing about so I really did not know what to expect. After I boarded the *Queen Elizabeth,* I was shown to my cabin and met the two other girls that were to share it with me. One was a GI bride who had met her husband when he was stationed in England and the other girl was traveling from Ireland to Boston to stay with a cousin. I have no idea of the destination of the bride but I clearly remembered the name Boston even though I had no idea where it was located. I do not remember the names of either of these girls, but they were congenial companions.

The *Queen Elizabeth* was a magnificent ship, and this was an incredible experience for me. It was November. After we left Southampton we sailed toward Cherbourg past the coast of Normandy. The Channel Islands were just a few miles to the south. The English Channel was not in a welcoming mood and even this great and glorious ship rolled and tossed through the night.

My bunk had a small round porthole window and I remember looking at the frothy waves tossing furiously against the glass. It was not an encouraging sight. The next morning we struggled up the steps and corridors clinging to the ropes on the stairs, for breakfast, and it really was a struggle. Finally we reached the dining room and our assigned table. We found that the sides of the table itself were up and that the tablecloth was wet. This was to prevent the plates and the food from falling on our laps. The seats were chained to the floor to keep them in place. We met our fourth companion for our meal times. She was a lady from Akron, Ohio, probably in her fifties. She wore a black Astrakhan fur coat. This fur was named after the city of Astrakhan, which was in the USSR. It was a loosely curled fur from lamb pelts. Our table companion was wearing a black one and it must have been very warm. I had seen coats like these in the '30s but do not recall having seen any since. She was friendly and talked about her hometown Akron in Ohio a lot. However, what I shall never forget about her is that each and every morning she agonized as to whether she would have one or two eggs for breakfast. I was fascinated, having just come from the war and rationing in England. I did not understand her problem. Perhaps she was way ahead of medicine and was thinking of her cholesterol level. Actually I think that I remember it was the calories that worried her, which was just as unbelievable to me. Calories in my experience only related to diabetic diets. We had no sooner eaten one egg for breakfast than we realized that we were all about to part company with it.

My cabin mates and I made for our bunks and we were all very sorry for ourselves. Not long afterward, the purser knocked on the door. He insisted that I get up and go on deck sit in a deck chair and stay there. I would be served a cup of hot broth and I was to drink it. I thought he was crazy. Actually, the advice was therapeutic. I never had a trace of nausea after that. The GI bride vomited so much that she was placed in the ship's hospital and we saw very little of her after that. I have often wondered about this thin and frail young girl and if she found happiness. The girl from Boston probably did well. It would be nice to know their stories.

The sea continued to be uncooperative. The decor of the ship was elegant. The main staircase was regal and fashioned in beautiful wood. Perhaps it had been refurbished after its wartime duties ferrying troops across the Atlantic. I am not sure when it was launched or put into service. It certainly was a world in itself. I do remember we were in a race with the new liner named the *United States* which, it was said, was the fastest ocean-going liner in service at that time. It could make the crossing in four or five days. Many years later I had the thrill of going on board the *Queen Elizabeth* once more. It was berthed in Florida and used as a tourist attraction. I tried to find my cabin, but the corridor was cordoned off. It was sad to see it that way, but I am so glad that I had the opportunity.

The weather was cloudy and rough for most of the five days. We took walks around the deck, whenever we could but it was cold and windy and the air was salty. I tried not to look over the rails too often. The ocean seemed so powerful and threatening. Drowning would not be my choice of departure from this world.

I shall never forget the ship's post office. I mailed a card to my mother and that seemed to be amazing to me because it connected us to land and we seemed to be so far from anything except the ocean. We were allowed to take a tour of the first class lounge and Sunday worship was held there. I went with my Irish companion and it seemed to be non-denominational. I was curious to see the swimming pool, but it was deserted and the water was sloshing up and down with the movement of the ship. I left it as soon as possible. It seemed to be so eerie.

The meals were plain. I saved all the menus for many years, but they have disappeared somewhere along the way. They were really attractive as I recall, and British cuisine was served so it would not have been unusual for me. If there was entertainment, it is only a vague and uncertain memory to me now.

The tension and excitement picked up as we were close to New York. Finally, it was the day of arrival. I stood on the deck on a misty gray day waiting for my first sight of the United States. It seemed to take forever but eventually there she was, the Statue of Liberty.

I saw the skyscrapers in the distance. However one prepares oneself, it is impossible to imagine one's first sight of the New World and I suspect it is unique to each individual. It is ours and forever ours alone.

Gradually we slid into the dock. This giant of a ship was handled so well by the expert crew. Would you believe it, the *United States* had beaten us and docked a few hours earlier. It had already disembarked its passengers.

The engines stopped and there was this general rush to land. The immigrants were separated from the Americans and the immigration officers came on board. I, however, was not with the other immigrants. I was met by Mr. Mulholland, who worked for the Port Authority of New York.

Mr. Mulholland had been a teacher at one of the Catholic schools in Jersey. Originally, he was from Ireland and had taught all of my mother's family. One day he surprised everyone by marrying a young lady who was also a teacher. They emigrated to America. He met every one of the Healy family for many years as they arrived in New York, meaning my grandparents and aunts and uncles. This time it was me. I came ashore with the American citizens, so I never saw my cabin mates again.

As we went down the gangplank and were about to step on American soil he told me to kneel down and kiss the ground. I looked at him in horror and I refused.

CHAPTER EIGHT

First Impressions

I shall attempt to record my impressions of America and Americans as I saw them at that time. I sense I may have sounded rather negative at the end of my last chapter. Nothing could be further from the truth. It is important to mention that I had no point of reference. Everything was foreign to me and I had no one to sound out. Everything moved so fast. I had no idea that thousands of immigrants had come to America in search of freedom and a better life. Consequently, the idea on kneeling down to kiss the ground seemed outrageous to me. Sort of like an act of treason. I set foot on American soil at approximately 11 a.m. on Wednesday the 26th of November 1952. It was the day before Thanksgiving. When Mr. Mullholland and I finally reached the dockside, I had my initiation into the workings of a labor union. The dockworkers were on strike. A heavy trunk is not lifter friendly. I believe now that the trunk must have been shipped from Jersey to Southampton and transferred to the ship. I could not possibly have had it with me in England. It was heavy and indestructible and whatever it weighed multiplied as we looked at it on the dock.

It was a damp and gloomy November morning. People were rushing about and frantically trying to find their luggage and get a taxi. Mr. Mullholland must have taken care of everything because I have no memory after that. The bright yellow cabs startled me as they darted through the traffic. They were so different from the black London cabs that were a tradition. The UK cab drivers were really quite distinguished, a breed all their own. They were especially respectful of London hospital nurses, always helpful and, in a way, protective. The yellow cabs appeared powerful and in command of the streets. The police uniform was a shock. In Jersey we had "Bobbies." The police I saw in front of me were rather intimidating and their caps for some reason made me uneasy. If they carried guns, I never noticed and I am not sure that I would have expected anything like that.

Mr. Mullholland took me to lunch and he ordered "Chicken on a bun" for me. I had never seen a hamburger bun and I did not know that I was supposed to pick it up with my fingers. Major shock eating without a knife and fork. I made sure that when I ate hamburger buns in the future I ate it with the traditional filling. I have never eaten chicken on a bun since November 26th, 1952.

Probably the WWII G.I.s had a similar culture shock in England during the war. I excused myself and went to the ladies room. This was a major shock. First, they were free, unlike England where one had to place a penny in the slot to open the door. I wonder if the words "spending a penny" evolved from this. It is not uncommon in England or Jersey to say that one has to spend a penny when one has to go to the bathroom. By this time I was alarmed, wondering in what kind of a place I was. The stalls were open at the bottom and I could see the ladies' feet! For all of my life in Jersey and in London, the toilets were completely enclosed. I was amazed and shocked. In reality, these were standard toilets.

Mr. Mulholland took me for a walk up 5th Avenue and showed me the Empire State Building. I do not remember the rest of the afternoon. By early evening it was time for me to take the train to Detroit. We walked into Grand Central Station. It was impressive. There was a choir singing Christmas carols on a platform and I was amazed, as it was only November. Why, I wondered, were they singing Christmas carols? I remember going through the gate to the trains. The ticket porter was wearing yet another style cap. I next remember it being dark outside and we were on our way. The train was crowded with servicemen, but I did not move out of my seat. I paid 50 cents for a pillow and tried to sleep. Actually, I handed the conductor a $1 bill and he gave me change. That was my first purchase with American currency. My Aunt Winnie had sent it to me. I do not remember the value, but it certainly provided a feeling of security. I think that it would have been difficult to obtain dollars from the banks in Jersey and England because of the stringent currency restrictions in place at that time.

I think that I dozed on and off during the night. The train came to a screeching halt at one stop. I looked out of the window and I could see the snowflakes falling gently in the lamplight at the station. This moment has remained etched in my mind for all of these years. We were in Albany, New York. It was almost like a scene in a movie. The rest of the journey was a blur.

It was an overnight trip and early in the morning the train pulled into Detroit. I had arrived in the Motor City of the world. Detroit is a sprawling city shaped like half a wagon wheel with its hub on the Detroit River. The center spoke is Woodward Avenue, named after one of Michigan's early Governors, and divides the city into east and west sides. It runs north a mile or so to the New Center area where the principal landmark is the gold-topped Fisher Building (named for the designers of auto bodies). When I arrived that November there was a huge construction project which later housed the City Building. I suppose I was a kind of modern day pilgrim arriving on Thanksgiving Day. Later I learned about the Thanksgiving parade and that Father Christmas was known as Santa Claus.

I got out of the train and in an instant the platform was deserted. My aunt had told me to wear a green ribbon and I certainly was not going to do that. No one was there, so I hoped I had got off at the right station. For a brief moment I felt quite lost. A kind black man, a "Red Cap," came up to me and I told him my story. He told me that the platform I needed to be on was upstairs. I felt like he threw me a lifeline.

My prior experience with platforms was in England and on the Continent and there was only one platform in those countries. He guided me to where I needed to go. I was not used to black people, but first impressions are important and I am still grateful for his kindness to me. When I reached the upper level, I looked around and saw no one that I recognized from the photographs.

The anticipation of meeting new family members is a unique experience. The relatives were all looking for the green ribbon.

Finally, my cousin's husband found me. My Aunt Winnie and Uncle Al were much smaller than I had imagined and goodness only knows what they thought of me. My cousin Joan was holding what I thought was a box of toilet paper. It was a box of Kleenex, which just happened to be the same size and shape as Jeyes toilet paper in England. She had a dreadful cold and a red nose to go with it. That Kleenex box broke the ice and we all laughed about it.

We went out to the car. It was bitterly cold and it was snowing. We drove through the downtown area of Gratiot Avenue in Detroit and I thought it was the ugliest place on earth. All of the years that I lived in Michigan that particular section of Gratiot Avenue never seemed to improve.

It was Thanksgiving Day and a new holiday experience for me. A furnace heated my aunt and uncles' house and the heat seemed to be overpowering. I had arrived in a climate that forbade opening the windows in the winter.

I was about to experience my first Thanksgiving. In Jersey, we ate turkey only once a year and that was Christmas Day. My aunt, in addition to meeting me at the station, produced the traditional Thanksgiving meal. Two of their friends arrived to share it with the family. They kindly brought me a bunch of flowers that my aunt had placed in my bedroom. They were big, heavy-set people of German descent. I seem to recall that they made their ethnic origin clear to me. They helped themselves to not just a serving but a mound of food the likes of which I had never seen before. When they picked up the drumstick with their fingers I could not believe my eyes. If the *Queen Elizabeth* had been docked nearby I would have gone back. In fact, that night I said to myself, "What have I done?" I never did feel comfortable with those two friends and I think in part it was because they were of German descent. They, of course, were very proud of their heritage, but it was still too close to the memories of the Occupation for me. Both Anne and I encountered the "ethnic" question many times and we wondered what we were being asked. This was totally foreign to us.

127

My aunt and uncle could not have been kinder to me and in recording my impressions they were simply as I saw and felt them to be at that time. I am not sure that I could have voiced them. Perhaps they were in my subconscious. I really cannot explain this, but these impressions remain in my memory. The first night, I really felt the climate change. It was cold. The next day my aunt took me for my first bus ride to a store named Federals and bought me an eiderdown for my bed. Very soon after that she introduced me to the wonderful world of the J.L.Hudson department store. What a marvelous experience. It was winter and cold and snowy, so my aunt also introduced me to boots that fitted over my shoes. I soon discovered that one of the nuisances of Detroit winters was having to wear those boots day after day.

As a little girl I had worn a lot of American dresses. My aunt was also my Godmother and, with the exception of the war years, had sent me some very lovely gifts. Most often it was clothing and sometimes it was toys. Before the war she sent me a Shirley Temple doll, the now "collectable" model. Anne, in one of those mischievous quiet moments that children have, cut Shirley's curls off. She thought that the hair would grow back! Such a lovely little sister. Actually she was a menace, always getting into my toys. We were not best friends then.

During nursing school, I had some of my cousin's hand-me-downs. We were about the same size. It was fun to have different clothes and styles. Another attraction at Hudson's was the restaurant on the 13th floor. Chicken pot pie was one of the favorite dishes and another first for me. There was a more casual eating place on the mezzanine. I seem to remember lots of cakes there. One could spend all day in the store and never get bored. I was familiar with the large London department stores but everything was on a bigger scale at Hudson's. They had not only one basement but two! The toilets were nice, too. They were more traditional and I think that one had to pay to use them. Wherever I go, I survey the toilets. Just procedure for me. I always think one can tell a good housekeeper by the bathrooms and the trash can containers. Please use plastic liners and put the toilet paper on the roller the correct way. After revealing that, no one will ever invite me to visit them again!

Anne and I grew up in a very small and separate family unit. We always knew that Mother's family was in America, but that was so far removed from our lives. Most of what I knew about that far away country was from Shirley Temple films. I was now with my Aunt Winnie (my mother's sister) and Uncle Al. They had one daughter named Joan and her husband was named Bill. They could not have been kinder to me and they were easy to know. I realize now that although we were born in Jersey, we were from very different backgrounds. Joan and Bill, who were native Detroiters, were very good companions. I had other cousins, most of whom I met only once. One cousin, also a Sheila, took me to Greenfield Village soon after I arrived. She stayed overnight and I was so surprised when I got up the next morning that she had my aunt call in sick for her. I, of course, as nurse had to go to work.

Joan was a nurse and a graduate of Mercy College in Detroit so we had similar career interests but our nursing background was very different. There was a little dog named Jill. I have always loved dogs, and she was good company. She was definitely an important member of the family.

In the summer time we all went north to the lakes for a vacation. We stayed in a rented cottage. It was a very happy time. It was also such a relief to get out of the heat and the city. I know now that I am not a city dweller, but I tried to adjust and it was not easy. I could not have voiced these feelings at the time. I felt the same way about living in London.

My uncle was a plumber and he worked in the Fisher building in Detroit. He had severe arthritis and his work must have caused him a lot of pain. Steroids had just come into use and this afforded him much relief. He was a gentleman and never complained. Aunt Winnie was much more outgoing and laughed a lot. She was feisty. They were both active in their church, which was St. Edwards in Detroit.

My mother, her sisters and brother were products of a <u>strict</u> Catholic family. They were all born in Jersey, but were part of the Irish community in the Island. My father's family members were strict Methodists. They were an old Jersey family.

My parents, to be honest, were both tired of the rigid structure of both denominations. When they married, they decided to please themselves and they slept in on Sundays. My mother said she was relieved when her parents went to America. Her father, who she dearly loved, checked up on her at Mass each Sunday and, of course, she was no where to be seen. She was a bit of a rebel in that regard. I cannot speak for the Methodist religion, but the Catholic Church in Jersey in those days left much to be desired. It seemed to be extremely biased, and from my mother's point of view, unfair. Just as in every section of the human family, there were good priests and bad ones. My mother won a doll when she was a child and the priest made her mother give it to a child in another family. The reason stated was that this other family never went to church. She never forgot this. There were many other instances when she believed that Canon Hourigan treated her parents unfairly. One example is that her father had to get out of bed when he was ill with the flu to lock the church at night. Many years later, when she was dying and confused, she stuck her tongue out at Father Dale Fusek, our Pastor, whom she <u>loved,</u> when he gave her the sacrament of the sick. She said, "I won first prize." We knew that she was the hurt little girl again whose doll was taken away from her.

Anne and I were christened in the Catholic Church and, in fairness to my parents, they sent me to catechism. It all fell apart when I was about to receive my First Communion. Right or wrong, my Father decided to let us choose when we grew up. I think he was wrong, but he had some very unfortunate experiences with the priests. As a non-Catholic parent, he was treated like a second class citizen. They had to be married at the side altar in the church because he was a non-Catholic. He asked the priest who christened Anne how he earned his living and the reply was "By my wits, son." This appalled my father. Before my mother died I asked her if she missed her religion in those days. She said, "Yes, but I loved your father." My parents never really escaped their religious upbringing. Anne and I were brought up in a very loving but strict manner.

Anne and I received our First Communion in Detroit as adults. I must say that my aunt and uncle never made an issue of this and we made our decisions on our own. That was very good of them. It was Bishop Fulton Sheen who influenced me. I watched him on television. I found his talks to be inspiring and practical. He had a television presence that was very appealing.

Now, since Vatican 2, the church is a different place. The liturgy is encouraging. We are taught to love and to be of service to others. The rules are the same and they are tough, but the promise is brighter and the possibilities are endless. We all know we are not perfect, but the goal is never to stop trying. I do not think I would belong in any other church. So I am grateful to my aunt and uncle that they never pushed me. They were my Godparents so their restraint was admirable.

Back to impressions. My aunt never pulled the drapes at night and this made me very uncomfortable. Especially since there was a murder in the neighborhood shortly after I arrived. Murders just did not happen in Jersey in those days. I have always been fearful in the dark and have night blindness. The rare occasions they left me alone in the house during the evening, I was truly scared. Probably the long years of blackout had some effect, but we always closed the curtains at night at home in Jersey.

There was this curious custom of keeping the bread in the refrigerator and it was soft and soggy, not like the crusty bread that I was used to at home. The bacon was thin and in small pieces. The taste was the same; it just looked different.

Detroit had an extraordinary asset. It was Sanders candy shop. Their chocolate is delicious and their hot fudge sundaes are out of this world. I had a banana split once, but that was enough. Never tried that again. I ate a lot of ice cream when I came to Detroit. It was addictive and there were so many flavors. Now, of course, I belong to the low fat yogurt generation.

One of the first smells that I remember was of popcorn in Kresges. I used to hold my breath every time we went in there. I found the smell to be unpleasant. I am not one of these individuals who loves new tastes. In fact, I would go out of my way to avoid them. Some would say that I am set in my ways. I can handle that.

In fact this is what I love about this time in my life. I know who I am and I relish the freedom that this sense of self brings. It is as though I am standing in a portrait gallery and all around me are stages of my life. Some I enjoy and some I would try not to repeat, but it is impossible to be back in time and place as that same person. In writing these memories I have moved from Europe to the United States as if from one room to another. I am as curious as I hope are you, the reader, as to which door this adventure will lead me.

Soon after I arrived in Detroit and in spite of the boots and the eiderdown, I caught a horrendous cold. I spent the days on the couch wrapped in a blanket. I passed the time between blowing my nose and coughing, watching television. This is when I met Arthur Godfrey and Pillsbury cakes, which I think was what he was advertising. This was very different from the radio, or rather "wireless," as I had known it. Then there were Old Gold cigarettes and a game show, which did not interest me at all. Lucky Strike had popular songs and the singer I think was a Canadian girl. Windsor Ontario comes to mind. She wore a white blouse (TV was black and white) with a ribbon tied at the collar. I must have been the only viewer who did not appreciate Jackie Gleason and Co. The surroundings in their "honeymooners" flat were so depressing. The American humor was lost on me.

Then there was football and all those lines up and down the field. Baseball completely baffled me and I thought the uniforms were really strange. I was never a sports fan, except for tennis, but football was as long a way from soccer as baseball was from cricket. I learned to enjoy American football but rarely view it now. Strange how one's interests change. None of what I say is meant as a criticism but simply to explain how I reacted to this new environment. My cousin Joan and her husband Bill lived in Lincoln

Park at that time. My aunt and uncle were in the East Side of Detroit. The journey back and forth seemed to be endless.

Christmas followed soon after Thanksgiving and I was familiar with this festive season. Hudson's had exquisite Christmas displays in each window. It was a family holiday and one of my first away from home. I must have been over my cold. I have no specific memories of the day except that my aunt had a unique choice of wrapping paper - newspaper. This Christmas I did go to church with the family and it was midnight mass. It was so long. Practicing Catholics at that time were required to fast two hours before receiving Communion. I did not have to fast, nor did the family, because I was not a practicing Catholic at the time. Probably the thought of being alone at house was one of the motivators. We opened the gifts before going to bed.

1953 – NEW WORK- NEW COUNTRY

After Christmas it was time for me to go to work. I had a brand new social security number. I began to make applications and was accepted at St. Joseph Mercy. It was located on East Grand Boulevard. I was used to living in a nursing residence so this was a major change for me. I had to leave the house when it was still dark and take two buses. It was wintertime January 1953 so the weather was unpredictable.

What I remember vividly were the workers from Packard Motor Car Company carrying tin boxes. It was like a uniform. Later I found out that these were their lunch boxes. I began working in the pediatric ward. I was working with a permit because I needed to sit for the State Board examination. It was another adjustment. The unit was in a very old section of the hospital. There were cribs for the infants and, horror of horrors, youth beds for the older children. These were back breakers. No recovery room in those days and the postoperative patients came directly to their beds and they were often still anesthetized. Tonsillectomy patients were plentiful and they came back in record succession. Bending over these low beds trying to care for these children was very difficult.

I met some great nurses and they were helpful and kind to me. Charting was different. In fact, it was all new and I had to learn a new routine. Each nurse was assigned to her own patients and I missed the teamwork that existed in the British system. I survived probably because I was young. I sat for the State Board examinations in June 1953. The examinations were held in Lansing, another city, another new experience. I passed all of them except the psychiatric section. I had never had any experience or education in psychiatric nursing. In the UK, another two years would have been added to become qualified in mental health nursing. There were no wards for the care of the mentally ill in a general hospital.

I was on a lower grade of pay until I could become a registered nurse in Michigan even though I did the same amount of work. I was eager to become registered. I took six private lessons from Dr. Keller, a psychiatrist in Detroit. I repeated that section of the State Boards and this time I was successful. I am not sure if this says great things about the physician or poor things about the specialty in those days. This time it was held in a building near the Detroit Public Library.

I remember a little black boy, I'll call him B, was admitted with severe burns on both of his legs. He had been playing with matches. I was assigned to care for him. He was about three years old and I really loved him. He was a brave little boy and he suffered so much. He had to soak in the tub each day and we had to peel him away from the sheets. He went to surgery one day screaming "Sheila" all the way to the elevator. I remember his surname and over the years I have wondered what happened to him. If he is alive, he must be about fifty years old now I wonder if he is able to walk. I hope so.

The nurses in the unit were very good to me. One took me to a Red Wings hockey game, my only visit. Another took me home for dinner one Friday night. I was expecting fish but she was Polish and it was duck blood soup. After one sip, I asked for toast. She was gem of a nurse and she taught me a lot about being Polish. Another nurse, this time of Italian heritage, asked me to go to Florida with her for a vacation. The family encouraged me and I think that it must have been in the summer of 1953. I had travelled a long way in a few months. Jo took me home to her house one day. I was surprised that her mother was not fluent in English. Obviously, her mother came from Italy. They were a lovely family and Jo and I had a good vacation in Miami. It was again all different, but I was at the ocean again and it felt good to me. The hotel room was very damp. I suppose that I had grown up in humidity living about a quarter of a mile from the ocean, but I do not remember that kind of dampness, probably because the temperatures were not as high in Florida.

About this time I met a nurse who had a great haircut. She went to a Monsieur Charles who had his salon in downtown Detroit. He was quite a character in his yellow smock and purple cravat. He really was an artist and he styled and cut my hair for years. Gone were the dreadful permanents and my hair has been back to its natural state, straight, ever since.

After a couple of years, one of the pediatricians was looking for an office nurse. The nurses with whom I was working told me that this was a great kind of job and I would have every weekend off and I would not have to wear a cap. An office nurse was completely foreign to me. I applied and was accepted. It was as promised a five day a week job with the exception that I was required to go into the office every third Saturday morning to answer the phones. If needed, I was to call the pharmacy with prescription orders. There was a list for me to use. I found this to be a very stressful job and I was very worried about making a mistake. I mentioned not wearing a cap. Another employee was a lay person and she was certainly more experienced in the office than I was. One of her first questions to me was whether I was going to wear my cap. Interestingly, I did not wear it and she reigned supreme. I lasted only nine months in that job and never worked outside of a hospital again.

Just at the right time for me a friend of my aunt was to have gall bladder surgery. There were no recovery rooms at that time. It was common practice for friends who were nurses to "special" friends. As far as I know there was no checking of the credentials, but I could be mistaken about that. I went with my cousin Joan to "special" this lady. She did well. After the surgery the surgeon came out to the husband with the offending gall bladder in a kidney dish as sort of a show and tell. I thought that this was beyond belief. The gall bladder was not so insignificant after all. By the end of that day I knew that I wanted to work at Bon Secours. It was the best decision that I ever made.

Bon Secours deserves a chapter all of its own. It has a special place in my heart and I left there with great sadness after 22 years to move to Arizona. Bon Secours shaped my life.

CHAPTER NINE

Bon Secours Hospital. Part 1

In November 1953 my mother and Anne followed me to Michigan. Our home in Jersey was rented to some people who had returned from Malaya. We lived with my aunt and uncle for about two years. Mother and Anne were working in downtown Detroit. I had just begun to work at Bon Secours Hospital. My Aunt Winnie must have felt somewhat burdened, having three extra people in the house but she never complained. Both she and my Uncle Al had been extremely generous all of their married lives. My grandparents had lived with them when they returned to the United States in 1926 and had remained there until their deaths. I would describe my aunt and my mother as having strong personalities. My mother, the youngest member of the Healy family, had always held this sister in high esteem. She was much closer to her than to her other sister and brother whom she had not heard from for many years. My aunt left Jersey as a very young woman. My mother had lived all of her life in Jersey and her experiences, as a grown woman, were very different. My mother and her sister had shared childhood together and she always looked to her older sister, Winnie, as a role model. Inevitably there were differences and these began to show. How often it is said that two women in one kitchen does not work. It was time for Mother, Anne, and me to leave and move on as an independent family once more. We were afraid to tell them how we felt.

I was happily working at Bon Secours Hospital making friends who encouraged me to look for a flat closer to the hospital. I was still taking two buses to get to work but in an entirely different direction. We started to look in the newspaper and finally found an ad that seemed to be just what we wanted. When my aunt and uncle were out we called and took the bus to see the flat. We inadvertently left the open newspaper by the telephone and when we returned the atmosphere was decidedly frosty. We should have been open and above board. Communication, however tough, is vital. Although the friction smoothed over, the breach was never entirely healed. The flat was just what we needed and wanted. The owners lived downstairs and they could not have been better to us. So three Jersey women began our lives together as a family in America.

APRIL 1955 - APRIL 1977

If I were asked to describe the single most defining experience of my life, without hesitation it would be the years I spent at Bon Secours Hospital. I suspect that very few in this world have the blessing of the perfect job but that was my experience. Was it really perfect? Of course not, but it came very close. After my cousin and I had taken care of the family friend following her gall bladder surgery, I made an appointment for an interview at Bon Secours Hospital. I did not even know if there were positions available. I simply felt drawn to the place. Sister Mary Margaret interviewed me. She was the Director of Nurses at that time. The salary quoted and to which I agreed was $14.50 per day per eight-hour shift. That was $1.85 per hour. I accepted and I felt rich. Employment was pretty basic in those days. No mention of overtime pay, in-service education or orientation. I doubt that those subjects were on the horizon. Sister took me on a tour of the wards. That is where I met Sister Xavier. Sister Xavier is a petite little lady. In those days, she wore the original habit. Her dark eyes and her face were all that were visible. Sister just exuded energy. I shall never forget that first meeting. She was asking one of the nurses to work a double shift and the response was "Yes, Sister." That was a new one on me. Later I had many opportunities to answer the same question and to work a double shift. The double part, 7 a.m. - 11:30 p.m., was not so bad. The difficult part was unwinding, getting to bed and being up again for duty at 7 the next morning. The very first day that I walked from the bus down Cadieux Road toward the hospital I knew that this was where I wanted to be.

The hospital is located in an upscale residential area, north of East Jefferson Avenue and south of Maumee. It is a red-brown brick, three-story building, blending pleasantly with the houses in the neighborhood. By the time I arrived, a new wing had been added to the original structure. The Sisters were living in an old white clapboard farmhouse next door, which was their first residence on the site. The wards, or halls as they were known, had two wings. The hospital at that time had 165 beds. The services available comprised of an increasingly active emergency room, obstetrics (St. Ann's), pediatrics, operating rooms and four medical-surgical halls. The halls were named after Saints. They were St.Camilus, St.Marys, St.Michaels, and St.Josephs. Some years later, the recovery room was opened, followed by an intensive care unit (Our Lady's Unit) and in 1967 a coronary care unit. All of these additions were incremental as progress pushed all of us forward. Perhaps pushed is not the word. We were all eager to embrace the changes that would increase the quality of care for our patients.

The new section was more spacious and the rooms were brighter. I spent most of my time in the old section. It began to feel like home. What I had found was a new family. The atmosphere was warm and friendly. The staff was small enough so that very soon everyone knew one another. There was an absolute commitment to good patient care. The Sisters cared about all of us. Thanksgiving, still new to me, was a celebration. That is when I learned to eat two turkey dinners in one day. Christmas was celebrated solemnly and with great joy. Working staff on the holidays were not forgotten.

Grosse Pointe, originally settled by the French, was adjacent to the city of Detroit, which at one time was an old frontier post. Grosse Pointe began as a French farming community. It remains a particularly attractive area to this day.

Alexis de Tocqueville and his partner Gustave de Beaumont were aware of this French connection. During their journey to

America in 1831, they had sought out a French priest, Father Gabriel Richard, who had been recommended to them as an authority on Michigan and the surrounding wilderness. Detroit had been founded by the Antoine de la Mothe Cadillac. The area of Michigan was known to trappers, priests, and traders from French Canada. It is difficult to imagine this area of Michigan as a wilderness today. The order of Bon Secours originated in France. It seems appropriate they should establish themselves in Grosse Pointe.

From the very beginning this order of Catholic nursing sisters was different. Founded in Paris in 1824, 12 young women dedicated their lives to God for a special mission; to minister to the sick, the suffering, the aged, and dying in their homes, and to do so with compassion and courage. Also to comfort, to heal, and to provide *Bon Secours*, which means *good help*. Unlike other orders, these Sisters went out into the community. They were completely devoted to nursing and would care for anyone, whatever their circumstances. If that meant staying overnight, they would do that. In my opinion, this is what made them real and enduring. Life in France was not easy but through all the travails, revolution, and persecution, the Sisters were out there caring for the sick. Wherever they were needed, they were of service.

In 1881 a handful of Sisters crossed the Atlantic to Baltimore. They chose this city to build their first American hospital. The Bon Secours Hospital continues to serve the city of Baltimore today. In 1909 the first Sisters came to Detroit. They began their work in a house on Trumbell Street. By 1914 they were in a house on Mc.Clellan Avenue. It was from there that the plans to open a nursing home in property at Grosse Pointe began. Bon Secours Hospital evolved from these humble beginnings. Once more the Sisters began by going out into the homes in the community. Physicians in the area observed their skill and compassion in caring for the sick. They encouraged them to open a nursing home. The Sisters were living in a home on Mc.Clellan Street in Detroit. They moved into the old white farmhouse on Cadieux Road and built the nursing home beside it. The Sisters' work continued. Before long the physicians were asking for a hospital. Bon Secours Hospital became a reality in 1944. They quickly realized that they needed help and to this day rely on their staff to help carry on their mission.

The hospital prospered and attracted top-notch physicians who wanted the Bon Secours standard of care for their patients. I was first assigned to St. Joseph's Hall. Within an hour, I was sent up the stairs to St. Mary's Hall because someone had called in sick. I worked on that busy hall for several years. That began my life with Bon Secours. Apart from a nurse aide who terrorized all newcomers, I never looked back. As soon as this rather huge individual found out that I was a hard worker, she got off my case. When one is young and certainly in those days (1950s) one puts up with all of that kind of nonsense. What a waste of time. Looking back, we all worked hard but we had a lot of fun. No overtime pay in those days. We worked until the work was done. Did we adore all of the Sisters? Of course not. There seemed to be lots of them. They were visible in all departments. From administration on down the line. Each hall had their own Sister, also Medical Records, the Operating Room, Central Supply and the Laundry (located in a building next to the hospital). Who amongst all of us in those days can forget dear old Sister Luke delivering the mail? We soon found out who worked and who did not. Those were the days when the Sisters were on the ward sun up to sun down. They would disappear from time to time to the convent for prayers. This was a bit of a mystery to us. I think that we were a little bit in awe of the habit and even though the Bon Secours Sisters were very human, we knew that they were not quite like us. The Catholic church had not yet gone through the changes that came with Vatican II.

Some of the Sisters who supervised us were just young girls. I wonder if some of them were not just a little bit awed by the responsibility. Team nursing was in vogue then. I gradually got used to the system where one nurse was assigned to six to eight patients with an aide to assist. A good aide was an asset and I can recall many busy days that were enjoyable. There were no recovery rooms and certainly no notion of an intensive care unit and the concept of a coronary unit was years away. Recovering a patient from anesthesia is a time-consuming responsibility. No air conditioning to cool us during the hot and humid Michigan summers.

One nurse was assigned to pass out all of the medications and start and monitor all of the intravenous fluids, including the blood transfusions. There were 37 patients on St. Mary's and this was one busy assignment. This was the responsibility of the senior nurse on duty. As it always happens, one day the "medicine" nurse called in sick. It was on a Sunday and I found myself in this strange territory, the "medicine" cupboard. No unit dose in those days. There were dozens of bottles on several shelves. I made it through the day and went home with a fierce headache. After that I was assigned to be the medicine nurse. The regular nurse was on vacation. When she returned, Sister Lucretia, the head nurse, assigned her to patient care. I begged Sister to assign me back to patient care. The regular nurse was older and it probably was some time since she had done hands-on patient care. It was really tough for her. Later she was transferred to St. Camillus. I became the medicine nurse once more. It was sort of a charge nurse position. I got quite possessive of that little cupboard. The shelves were high. I spent a lot of time hopping up and down on the stool. I realize now that I liked doing the medicines because it was kind of a solo responsibility and yet I was part of the team. I work well in that kind of situation. Patients have some common reactions. When they see a new nurse with their medication, they carefully check to see if all of their pills are there. Actually, that is a wise move on their part, but it sends a chill through the nurse who immediately thinks that she has made an error.

I needed experience starting intravenous infusions. One of the physicians finally taught me the technique. He had a patient who had very difficult veins. Probably none of us enjoy needles piercing our skin. Sometimes the veins are simply hard to see. Red-haired, freckled, and blonde people have veins like that. Veins that stand out and look so easy to puncture are often ropy and they have an artful habit of sliding when the needle pierces the skin. Frail elderly patients who may or may not be on steroids have tiny veins that are very difficult. You, the reader, now know more than you ever hoped to learn about veins, but anyone who has experienced one of the above will understand exactly what I have attempted to describe. Starting IVs became second nature to me and I was always sensitive to the fact that this was not a pleasant experience for the patient. I hate needles even for a blood test.

The Sisters served all the meals themselves and there was a personal touch. They knew who liked extra potatoes or gravy, etc. All of the patients, diets and portions were individualized. The nurses carried the trays to the patients (modern thought would not agree with this). The patients prepared for their trays; the head of the bed was raised up in a comfortable position. It was so much more appealing. I know that this may seem quaint to hospital staff members in the 21st century, but I have seen trays delivered and placed on the over-bed table far out of the patient's reach. I suppose the back rubs have disappeared too. I am not indicting the contemporary ways, but I want to go on record in stating that the "good old days" meant something to the patients.

I was very fortunate to be assigned to the day shift. Sometimes there was a need for a 3 p.m. to 11p.m. fill-in nurse. This was infinitely easier for me. I think I worked a few nights and it was the same old story, work all night and awake all the next day. It was exhausting.

My stint on St. Mary's Hall lasted about four years. We were always busy and the beds were full. No such things as "o" days (being sent home without pay) if the unit census was low. I cannot leave St. Mary's Hall without mentioning Sister Lucretia. She is an exceptional Sister, totally dedicated to her community and to the patients. She worked along with us every minute that she was in the unit. We respected her. We thought that she was a redhead and she had freckles. The habit made the Sisters features a guessing game. Sister Lucretia was always cheerful and she worked right along with the staff.

Another individual was one of the housekeepers. I can see her clearly but for once I cannot remember her name. She had an accent and she was a widow. My sense was that she had seen better times. She was an excellent housekeeper and a real lady. I always felt that down the line she had had a better life. One day she was found dead in her bed. We knew that she had a heart condition. I recall other housekeepers mentioned that her apartment was immaculate. I was not surprised. That made a lasting impression on me. I missed her and have fond memories of working with her. We were a close group. It is worth mentioning that finding a person dead in bed was not unusual in those days. Cardiology had not yet made the enormous strides that were yet to come.

Another individual was Olivia Karle, a young German nurse who came to Bon Secours. She was my contemporary. The other nurses were older but very good to work with. I tried hard not to like Olivia. She was German and we had been on very different sides during the war. She was impossible not to like and we have been friends all these years. Exactly a year ago she and her husband visited me in Arizona. It was good timing because my little poodle died the day before. We had a lovely dinner and we talked about family and politics. We discovered long ago that we had much in common.

Mother, Anne, and I were enjoying living in our flat. The first night I cooked the dinner before they came home. I burned the potatoes and they were really burned! I was out of practice. I had not lived with them as a family since 1945. Nurses lived in the nurses' residence in the UK and in Jersey. Hard to imagine now, but we each put $7 in the kitty for food each week and we had money left over. Those really were the days.

The family in America took it for granted that we had come to stay. The three of us grew into the idea. We made the decision to return to Jersey in 1956 to sell our home. I am not sure that any of us gave this major change serious thought. We made the trip in March of that year. I worked 18 days in a row to get the time off. We flew Pan Am from the airport at Willow Run and I know that the plane had propellers and that it was a very long journey, obviously before the era of jet engines. In London, we transferred to a smaller aircraft for the flight to Jersey. As luck would have it, fog enveloped the Islands and we were diverted to France. Here we were all set to make our big entrance into Jersey in our American clothes and our dazzling return was forever lost. The other passengers made the best of the night and we joined them. We made it into bed just before daylight, were barely asleep when the pilots awakened us to board the plane immediately. We arrived in Jersey unwashed with swollen eyes and slightly hung over. So much for the grand entrance.

We stayed with my Aunt Rita, our father's only sister. Our renters were tea planters from the Far East. They had all but destroyed our home. Perhaps they were used to servants. It was a nightmare. Luckily, the furniture was in storage. We faced the difficult task of deciding what to keep and what to sell. Young and stupid, we persuaded our mother to put the Wedgewood tea service in the sale. She never forgot it and we always regretted it. The return to Jersey was very special. We visited old friends.

As for our home, where we had lived as children, the devastation was very painful. The wallpaper in the bathroom was hanging from the walls. The carpets were soiled. Woodwork was scratched. Neighbors told us that the renters had large dogs that jumped in and out of the dining room windows at will. The Aga cooker was choked with grease. It was impossible to understand how individuals could live under these circumstances.

The weather was cold and damp. We stood in the house. It seemed to reproach us for having left it to these dreadful tenants. I have often described my mother as having been born with a scrubbing brush in her hands. This was a lady who loved her home and took pride in it. It was always a home that one felt that it was okay to bring one's friends. The kitchen floor was scrubbed every day. When I got to the age where I could help, I was given an assignment. I had specific responsibilities before I was allowed to go out to play. They were to dust and vacuum the three bedrooms, clean the bathroom, dust and vacuum the staircase (including all of the banisters) and to vacuum the upper and lower hallways. I had this down to a fine art in record time.

Anne has other memories. Her duties extended to the drawing room and the dining room. She reminded me of a piece of furniture in the drawing room that had many nooks and crannies. The dining room had a lot of brass. Everything was dusted every day. We were never asked to clean the fireplaces in wintertime, but let me assure the reader that they were clean and polished to perfection. There was a difference in Anne's experience. She argued over everything; consequently, the more she argued the longer her list of chores became. I must have learned to play the game and Anne never did! Truth is everyone was afraid to upset her. Our immediate circle was my parents and Nanny and Didda. Nanny was the nurse who assisted with our deliveries and Edna (Didda) was her daughter. She was Didda because that is the way I pronounced Edna as a small child. They essentially were the only grandmother and family that we knew. Didda was Anne's Godmother. They enjoyed an especially close relationship. Christmas, birthdays, all of the important and unimportant days were spent with them at our house. When Anne was in trouble, which was often, she just went over to live with them and stayed until she cooled down. Their house was very close to ours. Nanny really liked her spunk. I was the timid one. I cannot say too strongly how lonely it is to be perfect.

We were always close to Aunt Rita (Dad's sister). She lived at First Tower, which was where the Le Sueur family had lived for many, many years. That had been the location of the Le Sueur building business. Our grandfather owned it. He was a skilled and creative carpenter. He died at 46 and our grandmother sold the business at a loss, probably taken advantage of considering her lack of business sense and being a woman of those times. She and Aunt Rita lived at First tower. She was a very good aunt, never married and took in lodgers and visitors in the summer after our grandmother died. My parents had many friends who we called Aunt and Uncle. Their children were like cousins to us. So this reunion was very special to us.

Our house was sold and we went to the formal proceeding which took place in the States Chamber. The proceedings were conducted in French.

I have included all of these details because I believe that they are relevant to our major life change. This was very difficult for our mother. Sort of like selling her hopes, dreams and memories. The ending of a life that was happy and fulfilled. As a homeowner and as one to whom a home is all important, I find these memories to be excruciating. We left the Island by air and flew to London and stayed with friends who lived close to Wimbledon, an area in England well known to Americans. Anne recalls that I cried all the way to England. I have no memory of this. Leaving Jersey has always been emotional for me. The taxi that took us to the airport for our return journey drove past Wimbledon. That day the old green building looked somber and ghostlike. In just a few months, it would come alive with tennis and the cheers of the fans. We flew back to the US. The journey was endless and exhausting. The plane, Pan Am, propeller driven, was very comfortable; it was simply the length of time. My aunt and uncle met us in Detroit and took us to visit my cousin. I remember how tired I felt. We probably had a large dose of jet lag, but we were back at work soon after we returned. Before we left Jersey, arrangements had been made for our belongings and special pieces of family furniture to be shipped to us. It arrived some months later and not an item was damaged or broken. Opening and sorting through these memories was a day that I shall never forget.

Back at Bon Secours, life went back to normal. I had to work several long stretches to make up time lost because we had been away for five weeks. Nursing duties were different in those years. I remember patients in oxygen tents. That must have been a miserable experience for them. Piped in oxygen, was not available so we had to cope with heavy oxygen tanks at the bedside. Portable suction machines also were placed at the bedside. The nurse needed to keep the patients environment as tidy as possible in order to give care. CPR was not on the scene yet. There were no living wills and I do not remember a code status being in place.

147

To the modern nurse, this will sound like chaos. Actually it was not and patients and their families were respected and received good care. Nurses had more detailed work which might be scorned now. No disposable or any other labor saving devices were available. Nurses were more satisfied and not as competitive as they are today. Family units were much more intact and there were generations that had always lived in Michigan.

For a period of two months in 1957, I was transferred to the postpartum ward, probably because of my midwifery skills and to fill a need at that time. I clearly remember the 4th of July that year. It seemed that everyone that was pregnant delivered that day. There were babies everywhere. We used drawers as cribs which were lined up on the counter. Years later I discovered a nurse who was one of those babies. She was working in the recovery room. How quickly we get old!

Carol Loeffler was a fine nurse and a lovely young lady. There was a young couple who had their first child, a son that July 4th. For some reason I remembered them. They were young and carefree. Again, many years later I admitted the father to the Coronary Care Unit. He was a pilot. His wife had not told him that their health insurance had expired and she was so worried. They were still the same happy little couple. The day after his discharge, I met him on an escalator in the J.L.Hudson department store. He was delighted to tell me how he had spent his first night back home. So much for doctor's orders regarding abstinence! He certainly kept the unit jumping. The unit was a four-bed ward. The first Coronary Care Unit on the East Side of Detroit. It was pretty basic but it worked.

The summer of 1957 I went to England and Jersey for a vacation. I flew alone. I do not remember the type of aircraft, but it was on BOAC, which I suppose was British Overseas Airways Corporation. I stayed with Uncle Bill (my father's best WWII friend) and he drove me to Yorkshire to visit Ida. She was married and had a small baby. The baby named Howard, was quite adaptable and we had a good visit. I remember one early morning she plunked him on my bed while she went to make the tea. I wasn't

148

sure what to do with this tiny little baby. Eventually the tea arrived and she retrieved him. A cup of morning tea in bed was a real treat. Now I would not even think of it.

Ida, Ted, and the baby, Howard, drove me down to London airport and I flew to Jersey. I stayed in a hotel all on the strength of $14.50 per day I suppose. It was glorious weather and of course the attraction was also being with old friends. We spent a lot of time in familiar surroundings - the beach. We changed into our swimsuits on the beach and I told them that this was never done in the United States. They all agreed that this was very funny. For the record, all that is necessary, is a towel draped appropriately. I do not remember the flight back to the States. Life at Bon Secours went back to normal. There were lots of photos to share.

In March 1958, Anne had a blind date with what turned out to be her future husband. I went to Florida on vacation. I had exactly $39 in my checking account when I returned and that is all that I remember about that year. The blind date turned out to be eventful: Anne was married February 1959. It was a cold, snowy morning. She was a beautiful bride and her dress was lovely. It had dozens of tiny satin buttons which were a real challenge. It was only when we saw the photographs that we realized that in my haste I had put my headpiece on back to front. I now had sole possession of our bedroom. That was a relief and I rearranged the room that very night.

Sheila with first defibrillator and monitor at Bon Secours Hospital 1966.

Sheila with three nieces: top is Sheila (age 3), bottom row left to right: Tricia, Michele (approximately six months old).

Sheila, Salem Harbour, 1960.

CHAPTER TEN

Bon Secours Hospital. Part 2

The years that I spent working on St. Mary's Hall were carefree. I must have been about 30. The unit, with 35 beds, was the largest of the six halls in the hospital and it was always full and busy. The patient population was male and female, with medical and surgical problems. The rooms were private and semi-private and there was a seven-bed female ward.

There was a Sister on day duty (hers was a 12-hour shift) and about six staff members on that shift. It was a mix of registered, practical nurses and nurse aids. Staffing was the same on the 3-11p.m. shift. Nights had one of each. I can recall several patients, even to their diagnoses and family history.

We really worked and I do not want the reader to be misled by the word carefree. It is possible to work hard and enjoy it. That is real teamwork. It was on St. Mary's that I worked the 18-day stretch in order to have time off to go to Jersey in 1956. This was the place that we celebrated my American citizenship. It was from St. Mary's that I became my sister Anne's bridesmaid. I have good memories of the place and the people in it. As the medicine nurse, I was responsible for starting all of the intravenous and blood transfusions. It was a busy assignment but it perfected my technique and no doubt the patients appreciated that. I remember that I would get to work early each morning so that I could order all the supplies. Bon Secours people will all remember Polly Ringle, a cheerful and capable nurse who worked on the 3-11 p.m. shift. She never lost her cool and she was one of the few people who were shorter than me. Small in stature, Polly was the kind of person we all admired. She was a fun person. I write of her in the past tense because Polly died of colon cancer a few years ago. For many years after she left St.Mary's Hall, she was in charge of the Endoscopy department. Polly might be described a real Bon Secours nurse.

About 1960 I was transferred to St. Joseph's hall. That was the original floor that I started on but was moved to St. Mary's to cover a sick call. It was located directly below St. Mary's and had a few less rooms. Some of them were converted into administrative offices.

I have never worked in a hospital or any health care setting where space and budget were not an issue. This was in a sense a promotion. I once again assumed the responsibility for the medications plus supervision of the staff. I replaced a nurse who had been promoted to night supervisor, a job for me like life in prison without parole! Many of the night nurses were mothers who were able to work nights because the fathers were home with the children. Divorce and single mothers were not yet on the horizon. Also, many of the staff were long time employees and had been with the Sisters from the start. The atmosphere was one of caring and togetherness.

I enjoyed my time on St. Joseph's Hall very much. His life-sized statue dominated the south entrance. One day, Sister Liborius, who I believe was the Superior at the time, stopped me in the hall and told me that she was giving me a raise in salary. I was so surprised it never occurred to me that I needed one.

Princess Margaret was married in England while I was on St. Joseph's Hall. It was May 6, 1960, according to the commemorative china cup and saucer in my breakfront. I do remember the day. I was working in the male ward and it was either on television or the radio. Selective memory is amazing. It can drive one crazy or warm the heart. John Glenn orbited the earth February 20, 1962. A group of us were standing in the nurses' station listening to it on the radio. These events happened during my time on St. Joseph's Hall.

I mentioned the administrative offices that were situated at the end of St. Joseph's Hall. Sister Mary Gertrude was the Administrator. If one can describe a Sister in these words she was the "first lady." She was a powerhouse and highly respected for her ability. She established the foundation for what Bon Secours

Hospital became and is today. Her office was in the last patient room on St. Joseph's Hall. If there had been a suite of rooms available, she would not have been in them. Sister was one of the early sisters to come to Grosse Pointe. She was out in the community in patients' homes caring for the sick and dying. That is where the physicians in the community noticed her skills. Sister was able to combine caring with financial expertise. She was shrewd and patient care was her priority. The medical staff respected her and often sought her guidance. In order to get to her office, she went past the nurses' station and she often had a smile for the staff. She never stopped to chatter and she never interfered, but I suspect she missed nothing.

She had been one of the Sisters living in the house on McClellan Avenue in Detroit. My grandfather, who came to Detroit in 1926 from Jersey, would do odd jobs for the Sisters. He died in 1947 when I was at the London. I never knew him and certainly never expected to be in the United States. Sister knew him and was able to give me a first hand account of him. Life is strange. His granddaughter, whom he never met and who grew up in an island so far away, would find herself working for the same Bon Secours Sisters.

The Bon Secours story is too long to be told here. It is important to remember that the Sisters were once part of a family just like the rest of us. I certainly was never interested in becoming one of them nor did anyone suggest it. They pressured none of us.

The election of John Kennedy is part of my St. Joseph's Hall story. One of our nurses, Virginia, was a staunch Democrat. One of the surgeons was not a believer. For days they went around and around, Republican versus Democrat. It was something to behold. It was all done in good faith and there was no animosity. It livened up the morning when he made rounds. I remember thinking that I was not going to tell anyone how I planned to vote!

Staff meetings became the order of the day. I am not a meeting person. I do remember hearing about a family in Ohio suing a hospital or a physician and I was shocked. I found it unbelievable that anyone would doubt our integrity. Those were different days and such a thing was unheard of. It was some time before lawsuits became a prominent fact of daily life.

It was about 1963 when the nurse who was responsible for the In-service Education programs resigned to pursue her studies for a master's degree. Until this day I do not know who recommended me for her position. When I was approached I did not know what to do. I really was happy where I was. With much misgiving I accepted the position. The title was also Assistant Director of Nursing. Job responsibilities involved were providing ongoing educational programs for the staff. Sister Francis Helen was Director of Nurses at the time. We shared responsibility for interviewing and hiring new staff. We developed a close working relationship. When she was transferred to start a hospital in Virginia, I thought the bottom had dropped out of the world. She had been so supportive and taught me a lot in that position. The duties involved some speaking before groups. The first time I got up to the podium and the microphone I felt my body turn to Jell-O. I managed to get through it. After some experience, I learned to handle an audience and do it well. The essential ingredients are being prepared, answering questions and knowing your subject. One can have fun with the group. To this day I really enjoy it.

The job involved more than the nursing department. The dietary department had to be kept up to snuff in order to obtain and retain their food handlers' license. I did some work with the housekeeping department. I learned to love all these unheralded people. Pretty soon I knew just about all of the employees. We put on a fair in the Science Hall. The fair was to encourage all of the departments to show the rest of us what each department had contributed to make Bon Secours as successful as it had become.

The event had a tremendous response. The hospital laundry staff sewed tiny little clothes for their booth. One of the nurses from St. Mary's Hall made a wax face mask of herself. She made a hole in the throat and (with a hidden kidney dish containing water) simulated suctioning a tracheotomy. One of the telephone operators stood in front of it telling me that she had always wondered what a tracheotomy was! It was a major effort and everyone left knowing that each one in every department was involved in patient care. Learning can be effective in a creative approach.

Somewhere along the line, someone suggested to me that I enroll in the nursing program at Wayne State University. Hopefully this education would give me a Bachelor of Science Degree. This I did and at that time the requirement was to complete the liberal arts section before officially entering the nursing program proper.

I was at Wayne State University during the Cuban missile crisis. I was on a staircase with group students listening to the radio. The memories flooded back in an instant. I was terrified of war. I enjoyed the liberal arts classes and I got good grades. I was very disappointed when I had advanced enough for the serious nursing part of the program. I could not fulfil the requirements for Chemistry, so I was advised to transfer to the community college for this subject. Point of fact was that I was totally lacking in this subject. It was obvious that I was unable to fulfil the requirements at that level either. The professor at the college told me what I really knew and that was that I was not qualified to continue. I was relieved.

Just before WWII and after I had left Mandalay, I had begun to learn chemistry. It was clearly not going to be my favorite subject. When the Occupation started, we were left with teachers who had not evacuated from the Island and who apparently did not teach chemistry. We had no materials and I am not sure if the occupying forces would have allowed it. Believe me, I never missed it.

When I came to the United States my impression was that a Bachelor of Arts degree was not well respected. Certainly not for a nursing program. I understand that. I believe, however, that any education can help a patient because the nurse is the richer for it. This would not be an asset for the career ladder or any of that good stuff. Unfortunately, that non-nursing degree did not qualify for tuition reimbursement. I should have pursued liberal arts because I enjoyed the subjects. This may shock the entire nursing profession. What I am saying is that this restriction was rather short-sighted. Of course, it was my responsibility to continue with liberal arts for myself alone; I simply never thought of it. And without financial assistance it was probably impossible.

During my tenure of In-service Coordinator, I spent the summer months relieving the pediatric staff for their vacations. I enjoyed the children. Starting the intravenous infusions was a challenge, especially for the babies. At that time the site of injection was the babies scalp.

Completely out of the nursing role, a group of us got together and went into show business of the most amateur kind. In fact, we put on four performances. It was hilarious. Any staff member could join and did. Jim De Rousse, a surgical technician from the operating room, and I, were the producers. The rehearsals were so much fun. To describe us as amateurs is the understatement of the century. We all put our heart and souls in it. Rehearsals were after duty hours. Sister Francis Helen would roll in a cart full of food for us. The Sisters were so supportive. That is why I say they were special. They encouraged us all to have fun.

The performances were as follows: 1, the dress rehearsal. Dr. Ira Downer, a photographer of much talent, came to photograph us. 2, Performance, was for the grey ladies (volunteers). They thoroughly enjoyed themselves. 3. For the employees. They brought the house down. 4. The final show was for the physicians and they were a tough audience. Frankly, some of them were stuffy. A few of the more relaxed and enlightened ones enjoyed our efforts. Eventually, one or two of the young surgeons joined us and that was very successful. We put on the Christmas show for about three years.

One confession unrelated to the events above needs to be made here. It was the day that President Kennedy was assassinated. Everyone remembers where he or she was when they heard the news. I was in the Science Hall with the members of the procedure committee. We were, believe it or not, revising the procedure for the care of the patient after death.

That night one of the final rehearsals was scheduled. Yes, I made them rehearse, but I let them off early. A fine example of an American citizen I was turning out to be. The date was November 22, 1963. I had lived in the United States 11 years but apart from the horror of the assassination, I was not affected so deeply as my fellow workers. I apologize to the American readers.

One more story before I leave the nursing office. It was almost time for Spring and, as it is so often the case, the weather played a trick on us. It began to snow and forgot that it was supposed to stop. The 3-11 staff began to call in. They could not get out of their driveways and the roads became treacherous. So we did what we always did in an emergency, most of the hospital staff who did not have to make it home for children, stayed on duty.

By the time the night shift was due, conditions were even worse. Staff that were able stayed on duty. The maintenance folk found mattresses and many slept on the floor in the Science Hall. Some of the nurses, and I was one of them, slept in the Convent. We worked the day and afternoon shift. I had never been in the Convent and as we were climbing the stairs with only a flashlight, we came upon a lifelike figure. To say the least, it scared us. It was a life-size statue of St. Michael. None of us had ever met him before. The Sisters were sleeping and we were convulsed with laughter as we crept around the corridors looking for our rooms. Well, there were no mirrors, no minor comforts. I was in a corner room that was so cold. All I had to sleep in was a patient gown. The patients are exactly right when they complain about them. The back simply does not stay closed. We were up early to go back on duty. Putting on the yesterday's uniform (that had already done double duty) was a grungy experience. Everyone pitched in to prepare the patients' breakfasts and we were thankful to see those who made it in the next morning. We worked through the day and dug our cars out to go home that afternoon. None of us ever saw St. Michael again in that location. He was resurrected and transferred to the new wing.

I believe that I worked as In-service Coordinator about four years. I reached a point when I longed to go back to patient care. I believe that I spoke to Sister Mary Gertrude about it. I got my wish; I was transferred to the Intensive Care Unit (Our Lady's Unit) as a staff nurse. Herb Weot, a long-time employee in the maintenance department, stopped me in the corridor and told me how much he admired me for stepping down. I explained to him that for me it was a step up. It was a step I never regretted.

THE INTENSIVE CARE UNIT

The Intensive Care Unit was a five-bed male ward that had been converted to co-ed. This was before the days of monitors. Portable suction machines and oxygen were at each bed. The oxygen tanks were gone now and the oxygen was piped in. Just getting those tanks out of the way was an improvement. The staffing pattern W were two registered nurses on each shift in constant attendance. On the weekends, it was staffed with only one nurse. If the unit was full and busy, a second nurse was sent in to help. Weekends off had become a factor of life in the nursing profession. The rotation was every other weekend off. The nurses were firm about that. The unit had a special attraction for me. It was air-conditioned in the summer. The patient population was mixed: male and female, young and old, medical and surgical. Surgical admissions were most often transferred from the operating room directly to the unit during the weekdays.

We began to admit more and more patients with heart disease. Their treatment was the traditional method, bed rest and medications. Thinking back to those days is like looking at a horror movie. Patients with an irregular heart rhythm often died in their sleep and were not found until the night nurse made rounds. That could happen even as the nurse turned away from the bedside. We heard of monitors being used and Cardiopulmonary Resuscitation (CPR) being performed at other institutions but we had not fully appreciated the value of CPR until such an emergency arose one night. One of the residents was called to the unit at exactly the right time. He performed CPR on a lady who had suffered a heart attack and she lived. This was really big news! The resident was a graduate of the

University of Michigan and I am not sure that they can claim the credit. He was great and that particular day was his first day at Bon Secours. As of this writing he, Edward Applebaum, is professor of head and neck surgery at the University of Illinois.

Mrs. J was in bed 5. She was a delightful lady and following her complete recovery she was able to make at least two trips to Europe. This success made it clear that CPR was vital and the right of all patients when needed.

Monitors slowly came into use. We started with an old Electrodyne monitor. The problem was that none of the nurses knew how to interpret the rhythms. The monitor had an alarm system so it alerted us to the fact that something was wrong. Often it meant that an electrode had slipped off the patient's skin. I must repeat over and over again that this was a new intervention in patient care. We felt quite up to date.

The next piece of equipment was a defibrillator, which had a small monitor. It was quite small and there was an external pacemaker that was totally useless. The procedure was to insert two needles attached to one of the cables under the skin on the patient's chest. The theory was that this would stimulate the patient's heart. Actually it just made the patient's skin twitch. Needles with metal hubs were mandatory because those with a plastic hub did not transmit the electric current. Bizarre though this sounds today, it was new technology.

The next step up was the temporary pacemaker wire. The first patient that I cared for with one of these in place was a Mr. K, again in bed 5. It was like having a nuclear device in the unit. We were so unsophisticated.

The most important lesson in these stories is that we were willing to take risks to better serve our patients. They also were pioneers.

An electrical engineer was admitted with a recurrent ventricular tachycardia. For the lay reader, this is a serious cardiac rhythm. This patient had not suffered a heart attack but had some serious cardiac problems. He, because of his expertise, had an insight into his condition. He was a gem. One evening he went into this rapid cardiac rhythm and was not doing well. By this time we had a chart on the wall which helped us make a basic identification of the various rhythms. Joan (Yuhase) Kettel was on duty and relates the story well. She called the patient's cardiologist and was attempting to identify the rhythm. When she said it was like a series of standardization complexes, the doctor assured her that he would be right over! She relates with much humor how relieved she was to hear his squeaky shoes in the corridor. Eventually, some weeks later this patient died. He taught all of us a personal and professional lesson. He placed his trust in us.

It is important to remember that this was very different duty for nurses. We were so fortunate to have volunteers who wanted to learn. Nurses were never assigned arbitrarily to the unit. The off-duty ICU nurses were called in if needed. It became clear that the nurses needed education. We arranged a series of classes. The chief of the Cardiology service, Dr. Robert Griffin taught them. He was an excellent teacher and kept it simple in a series of 8-10 lectures. These were offered in our off duty time and after his office hours. Joan says that he gave us a test and that we all failed. Undaunted, he started again. I do not remember this. The good news was that soon we became very good at identifying the rhythms. Defibrillation was not yet part of the picture for the nursing staff at this point.

One began to hear sounds like Code 99 over the PA system and that attracted a crowd: the anesthesia department and all of the house officers plus private physicians. I do not think that there was a Respiratory therapy department established at that time. A patient, Mr. G, was admitted to bed # 2 in ICU. He had a heart attack. Suddenly he lost consciousness. We paged his physician, Dr.Dutcher, and the Consultant, Dr. Griffin, both responded. The patient was hooked up to the EKG machine. The manufacturer was the Sanborn Company. That is going pretty far back, but this piece of equipment was used at the time. Dr. Griffin proceeded to defibrillate the patient once or twice. There was no response and the situation was deemed terminal. He handed the paddles to me and said, "You try." This I did. In my excitement, I had no memory of what I had done, so I asked to do it again. Through no talent of mine I delivered the electric shock at the crucial time in the cardiac cycle and the patient's heartbeat converted to normal sinus rhythm.

The patient had cerebral edema (swelling of the brain) for a couple of days, but he survived. What I had done was out of the scope of nursing practice. I looked up to see Sister Justine, the Superior, standing in front of me. How she made it up to the unit so fast I never knew. I could have been fired, but not today.

Mr. G, was a fighter and he followed his doctor's orders to the letter. He returned to work and walked 40 blocks a day. He saw his daughter married and his grandchild born. The decision was made, in light of the evidence of CPR and the successful defibrillation, to plan and open a coronary care unit. The introduction of intravenous Lidocaine followed. I remember taking the order over the phone. Until then intravenous Lidocaine solution was used for patients with intractable back pain. I remember I repeated the order thinking I was not hearing correctly. Back then there was no accurate way to regulate the number of drips per minute. If we had failed to try, the advances in care for these patients would have suffered.

The Michigan Heart Association had just begun Coronary Care classes for nurses. The Department of Medicine recommended that I be sent. I was in the second class. I know that I was the only one in the class to have defibrillated a patient. It was great. From the very beginning, I had enjoyed caring for these patients. I was placed in charge of the planning for the nursing role in establishing the first coronary care unit on the East Side of Detroit. When I returned from the class I shared what I had learned with the other nurses.

THE CORONARY CARE UNIT

A busy and successful hospital always has a full patient load. The battle for beds between the medical and surgical departments was on going and fierce. I fear that will never change. Patients wanted to come to Bon Secours Hospital. The innovation of the ICU had irked the surgeons because all they saw was loss of surgical

161

beds. General surgery patients did not need the level of ICU attention. When the decision was made to take another ward for the exclusive use of the medical department, the surgeons were outraged. The nurses took some of the flak for this but all we could do was smile, but not too broadly. When, however, one or two of their peers were admitted to the Coronary Care Unit the surgeons' passions cooled. I know without a doubt that the 12 years I spent involved with the Coronary Care unit at Bon Secours unit were the happiest and most meaningful of my 48 year career. It was beyond satisfying. If when my life is over and I am asked to give an accounting of myself I shall say that this was my best effort to aid others. We were able to help so many people and we forged ahead in an entirely new frontier for the nursing profession. It was teamwork and it worked.

The planning kept me busy and I learned a lot. Our first unit was very basic. Four beds and the style of an open ward fish bowl design, men and women. Any physician had privileges to admit, but a cardiology consult was required. We had routine orders and in the beginning we had only one registered nurse on duty for each shift. We willingly worked six days a week to get this new venture started. Sometimes you just have to make things happen.

We opened the unit Thanksgiving Day 1967. We transferred three patients over from ICU and they were really proud that this Dr. Griffin, chief of cardiology, had chosen Hewlett Packard monitoring equipment. It was state of the art. After ICU, it was like luxury. We had an important feature. When the alarms went off, there was a print out and so we had a record of the event. Dr. Griffin made slides of the monitor strips. I used them to teach the nurses. I had the advantage of knowing the patients so I could make the strips come alive. This is what the nurses needed: realistic situations. Many hospitals failed to add a printout in their units which made it very difficult for their nurses. At Bon Secours we were able to share our experiences with other nurses in the state. They were hungry for direction. Our equipment had been donated by generous benefactors; William and Lynette Holden,. The unit bears their name.

I have worked with a lot of great nurses during my career, but none can equal the group that started in CCU. We learned, we laughed, we cared and we supported one another. We were in the right place at the right time. The Sisters were proud of us and generous with their praise. It was a joint venture with the medical service. Everyone looked on Dr. Griffin as a leader. He got a lot of calls.

Sometimes situations were a little sticky before the rules that eventually regulated the unit were established. The nurses were often more skilled in understanding the cardiac rhythms than some of the physicians. It depended upon how the doctor felt about him or herself. Some were threatened and some asked for help. It required tact on the nurses' part. I was not too patient most of the time. I know that I tried to be patient. It is important to point out that the idea of nurses becoming "partners" in care with the physicians was unknown in the past. We all felt the change in the relationship. We knew that they counted on us and we worked hard to live up to their expectations.

The Coronary Care Unit was a relatively small room but, in some ways, that made all of us closer. From the beginning we got the patients up to the bathroom. But obviously, not if they were unstable. Bedpans are tricky to maneuver, even for a healthy person.

The Michigan Heart Association did not have a building. When its officials approached us Dr. Griffin agreed to let them use our facility. It was convenient for our nurses to take the class in familiar surroundings. In addition to that we took nurses from other hospitals to work along with us. We taught them on the job. There was no charge for this, and as far as I know no risk management considerations. How times have changed.

At that time I met Eleanor Darcy Peterson, the nurse coordinator at the Heart Association. That was the beginning of a deep and abiding friendship that lasted until her death 30 years later. I worked with her for many years. Eventually the association had a new building so the classes met there. I continued to teach at the Heart

Association. Joan Kettel assisted me and carried on teaching when I resigned to move to Arizona.

At the beginning, I mentioned we helped a lot of people. It was so gratifying to see people get well and return to their homes and families. Nurses were able to report better information to the physicians. We were able to educate the patients and their families. The nurses learned to use their stethoscopes and to avert serious complications. I remember one cardiologist, Dr. Hugh Henderson, telling me he was amazed to get a phone call from a nurse telling him that one of his patients had a friction rub. This is a heart sound sometimes heard when the heart muscle is damaged, as in a heart attack. It became routine to defibrillate patients.

One case that comes to mind is very instructive in that it shows the development of standardized routines. One Sunday morning a woman in her early 40s was admitted. Women were not thought to have heart attacks. Her cardiologist, Dr. Griffin, told me that her EKG looked suspicious so he thought it wise to admit her purely for observation. She was in Grosse Pointe for a wedding. It was fall and the Detroit Lions were playing at Tiger Stadium. She had lunch and settled down. Soon after 2pm. I noticed that her heart rate was slowing down. Sure enough, she was going into heart block. That means that the normal pathway for the electrical impulse to travel through the heart was blocked. This was life threatening. We tried all the answering services but everyone was at the game. We needed an order for atropine (a drug which speeds the heart rate). We reached Dr. Jacques Beaudoin, a thoracic surgeon (he was a former NHL hockey player) who inserted the pacemakers when needed. As usual he came over right away. He ordered the atropine. The heart rate increased and all was well with the patient. Following that event, Atropine was on our routine orders. Women did, and do, have heart attacks. There are so many patients in my memory bank. We lost some but it was pretty difficult to die in our unit. No longer did we find patients dead in bed. We were right on top of it and monitored them constantly. At that time patients did not live long past the age of 65. Every time I hear the controversy about Medicare

I understand why. We changed the picture and the program. Patients live longer. Advances in patient care have increased the cost of saving lives. We changed, and I mean all of us, at that time. I know that it was worth it. Sixty-five seems younger to me every day.

Before I left Bon Secours we had moved the CCU to larger quarters. We had an eight-bed unit fully equipped; once more it was state of the art. It was a model unit. Each patient was in a separate room. They were visible to the nursing staff at all times. I worked once more with the architects. That is a very important component in planning. I was determined that the electrical outlets were placed in functional locations for the nurses. There was a built-in defibrillator at every bedside. We continued to have the latest Hewlett Packard equipment. A word about service. Our original defibrillator was manufactured in California, which was not convenient from a service location point of view in Michigan. Hewlett Packard was in Detroit. They were just super with service and were terrific people with whom to work. I had a long association with them. In the beginning, I must have driven them crazy. I believe that when all is said and done we all learned together and appreciated one another.

For me it was the opportunity of a lifetime. I travelled all over the state of Michigan with the Heart Association. I was involved in programs for physicians as well as for nurses. I shall never forget one program. The speakers, physicians from all over the country, were highly regarded specialists. Eleanor paid me the same honorarium. It was quite a windfall. The Good Sisters never asked and I never told.

The Coronary Care Unit meant so much to me. The patients and their families were special people, so appreciative for this new technology. How easily we forget. I said at the beginning that at Bon Secours Hospital I found the perfect job. I hope that the reader will perceive some of that from my story. Words seem so inadequate. I shall close this chapter now and dedicate it to all of the nurses who, many years ago helped shape and change the care of cardiac patients, and my life. It is their story as much as it is mine.

CHAPTER ELEVEN

American Citizenship And The Americanization Of Sheila

The legal process was relatively easy. The Americanization took a lot longer. The criterion for application was five years residency. I remember very clearly that my aunt and uncle signed to accept responsibility when I entered the United States. Most of what I remember is the five-year waiting period. The process involved a series of maybe two or three classes about the country. I seem to remember a small informational booklet, but this may not be accurate. There must have been paperwork, but I have no clear memory of that either.

As a holder of a green card, I had reported each year at the Immigration Office on East Jefferson Avenue in Detroit. I had been employed for just over five years. After our visit to Jersey in 1956, I once again entered the US with my UK passport.

I was notified to appear downtown Detroit for testing. I have a vague memory of a small office and the immigration officer. He was very serious and I was very nervous. The only question that I can remember was "Who is the Governor of Michigan?" It was G. Mennen Williams. He wore a bow tie, had a large smile and a flat haircut. He really looked and sounded like an American to me at the time. I made it through the test without any problem.

When it was my sister Anne's turn, she was asked how many men were on a baseball team. We thought that this was a dumb question then and we still do today. To be honest, neither of us knows to this day. Anne has only been to one baseball game and she says that the most memorable part about it was that she sat next to NHL legend Gordie Howe. He was a very nice person. All through the game people were coming up to him and asking for his autograph. He was amiable and patient with all of them. Anne did not ask him; she felt that he had enough interruptions. My baseball experience was at one game also. A French friend was visiting. She wore a low-cut sundress and no bra. There was a continual stream of males, including the players, who found her to be the most desirable attraction in Tiger stadium. I was bored stiff.

Some weeks later I was scheduled to report for the final ceremony. I was on duty at Bon Secours Hospital and I took the bus to Detroit. I was really excited. I expected to become an instant American.

March 18, 1958, I stood with a small group of immigrants in a Detroit courtroom. I was by myself and I believe I was the only person that was a British subject. There were some Asians and the rest were Europeans. They spoke with an accent. What I mean is English was not their first language. Judge Picard was presiding. He spoke for a few minutes, explaining the seriousness of what we were undertaking. We swore to defend and obey the laws of the United States, to renounce our allegiance to our former country, and suddenly it was over. I left the building, caught a bus and went back to the hospital. It was such a let down. It all seemed so matter of fact. When was I going to feel like an American?

What I know now is that for me it was a process. I had survived five years of war and Occupation. I had lived in freedom for thirteen years and I had made many changes in my life. This was a serious commitment and yet I still felt that I belonged to Jersey. This was not a conscious feeling and I continued to move forward and in many ways the United States did feel like home.

When I walked in to St. Mary's Hall, I was stunned. The nurses' station had been transformed. Red, white, and blue bunting was everywhere. In other words, I found a true American reception. There are no other people on this earth with the generosity of spirit in accepting and welcoming a newcomer to their country. The American people really know how to party! It was overwhelming. We had been given a booklet for remembrance and everyone who walked by the nurses' station that day signed it: physicians, nurses, visitors even the patients. The ward appeared as if a presidential visit was about to happen at any minute. Somehow the medicines got around that day.

That evening there was a private party. I was given a small charm - an American flag. It was inscribed with my initials and the date March 18, 1958. That is a date that I shall never forget, certainly one that I never planned.

The official document was a certificate #8027533 and the petition was #263827. Both numbers have 27 in them, and that is the year that I was born. It must not be photographed or copied. It has always been in safekeeping. My certificate states that I received my citizenship in the Easter District, Southern Division U.S. District Court of Michigan. I was legally a United States citizen. The document also includes my vital statistics. I am relieved to read that I have only gained five pounds. I weighed in at 110lbs. This certificate is a privilege. Many would die for it.

The year was 1958 and I voted for the first time. I was very apprehensive; I never voted before. It was a typical November day in Michigan: cold, wet, and grey. I had been well coached about the procedure. I stood in line and watched all the feet, which was all that was visible from behind the curtain. When it came to my turn, my heart was pounding. I was worried how I would get in and out of the curtains. This was a major experience for me. I voted for President Eisenhower on the Republican ticket. He was an easy choice. He was the leader of the Normandy invasion force who had come to liberate us.

I knew very little about politics in any country. I had grown up in a conservative family. Winston Churchill was and will always be our absolute hero. He was the leader of the Conservative Party in England so I figured that I was a Republican. I had it all wrong. As a Channel Islander, I would not have been able to vote in England. The States of Jersey is not organized on a political party system and no distinction is made between "Government" and "Opposition," as is the case in the United Kingdom. The States of Jersey operates on a committee basis. I never remember my parents having the opportunity to vote.

All of these years I have been a faithful voter. The exception was the Johnson-Goldwater election. I was not sure about that and Arizona was just not on my map. Who could have ever imagined that I would live here? With one exception, I had voted as a Republican. For some years now I have been an Independent and neither the Republicans nor the Democrat have persuaded me to change.

I must be honest and admit that for years I had a kind of identity struggle. I have felt almost American at times. This has been self-imposed and is no indication of how I have ever been treated in this country. I confess that I have made many wonderful trips back to the Island. My friends introduce me as their American friend and this never fails to startle me. If we go on a day trip to France, I disembark from the boat directly in view of the house and the bedroom where I was born. I enter with the foreign nationals. That is a very strange feeling. One plus is that the immigration officers recognize my name and they can pronounce it properly. They always welcome me back to Jersey. That gives me a thrill.

I have also learned that it is much more than sounding like an American when I speak. Holding my fork in my right hand is a dead giveaway. I can switch to my left hand if necessary, but I rarely do. I think back to my first meal in Detroit and I remember thinking that Americans had horrible table manners.

Friends have no boundaries and mutual affection has no nationality. My friends are the mainstays of my life after my family. I just wished that they all lived closer to one another and to me.

When I am in Jersey, I know that I am different. I am much more confident and open. I wear American clothes and they are recognized around the world. Blue jeans have a universal language all their own - there is something about the cut of the American ones.

I have often been told that Jersey never lets her people go. I know that I also belong to the United States. It has been a tug of war for me. It is this "am I really an American?" I have always felt that anyone born in this country is a real American regardless of race, color, or ethnic origin. The real question is where would all of us be without immigration?

As an American, no opportunity has been denied me. I have achieved the American dream of owning my own home. I enjoy the American people, their openness and sense of humor. If I do not feel at home, that is my hang up, not theirs. My American pets have been one of the joys of my life. I have a genuine American family: my nieces and my nephew. Their names are Sheila, Tricia, Michele, Alison, and Matthew. They were all born at Bon Secours Hospital in Grosse Pointe, Michigan. I am grateful.

CHAPTER TWELVE

Adieu to Bon Secours Hospital and Michigan

Sometime in 1975 I transferred from the Coronary Care Unit to the position of Critical Care Coordinator, working out of the nursing office. Critical care included the Emergency Room. My responsibilities were primarily administrative. One facet of the position was assuring adequate staffing on all shifts. For the most part, the nurses had young families. One never knew when an illness or a family emergency would come up at a moment's notice and throw us into a bind. The exception being on the weekends when our responsibilities expanded to cover the whole hospital. Undoubtedly the down side of that position was the responsibility for ensuring that each area had sufficient coverage. The coordinators (I seem to remember there were about six of us) rotated all the shifts on the weekends. I dreaded night duty but found that the 3-11p.m. hours had many advantages.

It was a busy shift coping with emergency admissions and postoperative patients. There were more visitors and questions to answer, which often tested our ingenuity and diplomacy. Visiting hours ended about 9 p.m. Some visitors liked to linger but we eventually were able to persuade them that the patients needed to settle down for the night. There were treatments to be done and medicines to be given.

The upside of rotating on all the shifts was meeting and getting to know the many wonderful nurses and staff on the other floors, and ensuring that each area had sufficient coverage. The downside of the job was that the further one is away from bedside nursing, the harder it is to remain proficient. On the other hand, administrative positions are unavoidable and necessary. Life changes and so did mine. I had reached a fork in the road and it was time to make a change in my life.

My sister and her family moved to Scottsdale, Arizona in 1974 and she wrote about the good weather. My mother had retired and she found the winters were pretty confining. She did not drive. I would come home from work and she would be standing waiting for me with a cup of tea in her hand. Most of all she was missing her grandchildren. It was an agonizing decision, but I made it. January 1977 I visited my sister in Arizona and put a down payment on a townhouse, returned to Michigan and resigned from Bon Secours. I heard later that within an hour three people applied for my position.

I put the first house that I had ever owned on the market. There were still more bittersweet moments to come. When prospective buyers came to see it I found it painful. Having my own home is very important to me. It is said that there is a buyer for every home, and that proved to be true. When I moved into my house in 1971 the first thing that I did was to get a dog. I had wanted one for years. If there is the right buyer for every house it is especially true for a pet. I saw an ad in the paper and went to see a puppy. It was an instant match and he was mine. He had been named by the owners and I did not try to change it. His name was Beau. He was a miniature poodle and his color was apricot. Anne brought him to the house the day that we moved in. Beau was born in Sausilito, California so he was a westerner. I was about to take him back to the west.

I had a tremendous send-off from Bon Secours - deserved or not. There were many gifts and some awards. The technical staff at Hewlett Packard, whom I just about terrorized in the early days of CCU, arrived at my house with speakers for my stereo. They were a grand group of helpful people. The thought of new horizons was attractive, but leaving for them was unnerving. The good part about it was that we would be close to Anne and her family.

The moving company packed our house on June 1st, my fiftieth birthday, and I shall never forget it. It was a sad day watching strangers pack our belongings. The next day they loaded the truck. We slept at the neighbors and the next morning Mother, Beau, and I

173

set off for Arizona. Beau was a good traveller. He sat between us and as long as I was right beside him that was all that he needed. I needed him, too. The trip was uneventful. In Texas, a gas station attendant told me I needed new shock absorbers. I was driving a new Oldsmobile so I ignored him. We arrived at the Arizona border June 7, 1977. There was a mandatory stop when our car was searched for fruit, which may be carrying insects or bugs of some kind. Now that we crossed the border into Arizona, our lives as Westerners began.

CHAPTER THIRTEEN

Living in Arizona

Living in Arizona is different, almost unreal. In a way it is like being on vacation, but it is real life and it is different. That is not a clear description but it is how I felt when I first came to the State.

We arrived at the start of the hot summer months. That had the advantage of facing the worst and being able to look forward to the best weather that the winter months bring. In my opinion, the real winter months are December and January. The days are shorter and the nights much colder. The rest of the months the weather is very pleasant.

It is early November as I sit writing this part of the story. It is perfectly warm and sunny with clear skies with not a trace of rain. If I were in Michigan, I would be wearing winter clothes, the heat would be on in the house and perhaps I would be wondering when the first snowfall would begin. If I were in Jersey, the skies might be overcast, it may rain and I would wear winter clothes.

In retirement, I seem to wear shorts most of the year, sweats in the winter and dress formally if the occasion calls for it. It makes for a decidedly casual lifestyle. When I was working, I wore uniforms in the hospital, but for Hospice we wore our regular clothes. Living in the Valley of the Sun, I never need boots and the only reason that I have three raincoats is because I am a former Brit and the raincoats never wear out. I do own an umbrella, of course.

The houses are different. Very few have basements and they are constructed for the climate. The interiors are very much open in plan. An air conditioner is mandatory. There is a heater in the house. That is used to take the chill off the air in the winter early morning hours. One of the things one hears most from visitors and from those who have moved here is "No snow to shovel."

During the summer months we stay mainly indoors. The cars, stores, and public buildings are all air conditioned so even though we complain about the heat it does end and at this time of year it is hard to remember why we were grumbling. Arizona is an interesting state. It really does have something for everyone. There are mountains, lakes, the Grand Canyon, and the red rocks of Sedona. There are rivers that can fill the washes in a moment following heavy rainstorms, and which remain innocently dry and barren most of the time. On other rivers and lakes fishermen can find the catch of a lifetime. In winter, skiers flock to the north and higher elevations of the state, to slopes that they love. There is a large migration from all over the United States and from Mexico. The housing market is experiencing boom times. The high tech industries are well established. Sometimes it seems as though the entire population of the United States is moving here.

Traffic is not a lot of fun and always seems to grow faster than the freeways. Phoenix is becoming a major player in the sports world. There are three major universities: Northern Arizona in Flagstaff, Arizona State in Tempe, and the University of Arizona in Tucson. There are many community colleges, the largest being the Maricopa College district. It is the largest community college district in the United States. Mesa Community College in this district is where our group New Frontiers calls home. Theater and the arts flourish and there is every choice of cuisine available in the restaurants.

This is the world that I live in and if anyone had told me that I would be here I would never have believed them. When I moved here I bought a townhouse. Less then two years later I moved to a single-family house in a new development. I lived in that house seventeen years - the longest that I have ever lived anywhere.

When I came close to retirement I felt that I needed to move. I had two dogs but they were getting older and I did not want to live in that house alone. I cleaned the house from top to bottom and made sure that everything was in tiptop shape thinking that I would be all set for summer. The house had a large back, side, and front yard. In the seventeen years the trees had grown and I had long since needed help for all of it.

By chance, I found a condo (which I am told is a planned community and not a condo) that looked okay, but I was not impressed. I had just retired and so I was not in a hurry.

To end this long tale, my house sold in three hours for cash. I was in a panic, where was I going to live with two dogs?

Anne and I went out to see the condo. "What more do you want?" she said. Tuffy, Chip, and I moved in five weeks later. It has been a very good move. I enjoyed decorating all of my homes and this is no exception. It is very lovely. I do know how to make a home and that for me is very important. I am very fortunate.

The community is top rate and the neighbors could not be better. I am on the Board of Directors and (heaven help them) I am the secretary (women's work). They don't fool me. I remind all the nice men regularly. How many male secretaries are in this world? Not many! I enjoy visitors but not in the summer. Two classmates from England have visited in June and July not believing my warnings about the heat. Their English complexions turned to rosy red in an instant. The minute we stepped out of the airport to the garage area they knew that they were in trouble. Now they are believers. I warn all of them that toast is the only specialty of the house. No.73 is a very good place to call home.

CHAPTER FOURTEEN

Working in Arizona

Working in Arizona was different. I suppose that if one is going to make a change it might as well be a dramatic one. Michigan, was how I had seen and experienced the United States for 25 years. I had visited other states for vacations, but this was a major move. I had made a gradual cultural change and it was huge after being confined in Jersey's 45 square miles during the Occupation.

My nursing school was in the East End of London. I had never been in a city, much less lived in one, until that time. I did not particularly like what I saw of the East End. We escaped up to the West End at every opportunity. Each time I return to the city now I feel a thrill of pride. It has an aura of tradition and majesty. When I arrived in New York, so huge and so different with its air of urgency, I was acutely aware of the difference.

Finally, Detroit, a working city, lacked the polish of the other two but spoke loudly that the automobile was King. This was the Motor City of the world. I was about to make another change. When we crossed the border from New Mexico into Arizona I would be moving into a totally new working environment.

After our car went through the mandatory inspection for fruit or bugs at the border we drove on through the city of Flagstaff. We continued through the mountains and as we drove down into the Valley, we began to feel the increase in the temperature. It took us about three hours to reach my sister's house in Tempe, she lived close to Arizona State University. Phoenix, the largest city in Arizona, looked so new as it shone in the late morning sun. We passed Sky Harbor Airport in the center of the city, a site easily accessible to the whole area. The next day the family left for Disneyland, allowing us to stay in their house and take care of the pets while we became acclimated.

It was especially hot when we arrived. I spent a lot of time in their pool. The moving van took longer than expected because it went to Tuscon first. Eventually it arrived in Tempe. Beau and I moved into our new townhouse; my mother settled into a townhouse near Anne and family. It was the first time that our mother had ever lived alone. We were all living in the same city for the first time in many years.

Arizona as a state is moving rapidly into the future. Once thought to be a desert wasteland, Indian tribes have inhabited it for hundreds of years. Today the third largest Indian population in the United States lives in Arizona. The name Arizona is an Indian word but its meaning is unclear. It may mean a small spring, or land of springs.

Arizona is located in the southwest corner of the United States. Bordering it on the southwest is California; the east, New Mexico; the south, Mexico; and to the north, Utah. Arizona, New Mexico, Colorado, and Utah join together in what is known as the Four Corners area. Tourists to this site are able to say that they stood in all four states at once.

For hundreds of years the Indians lived undisturbed. In the early 1500s the Spaniards in Mexico heard stories of the vast riches to the north. They sent expeditions and the Indians passionately defended their lands. The Spaniards ultimately triumphed. The first white person to enter Arizona was a Franciscan priest named Marcos De Niza. When Mexico won its independence from Spain, Arizona became part of Mexico.

The civil war (1861-1865) brought great changes to the area. In the 1850s the settlers asked Congress to create an Arizona territory. Their requests were denied. Most of the settlers were from the south and their sympathies were with the Confederacy. After the defeat of the South, the Congress created the Arizona Territory. Its boundaries remain in place today.

December 27, 1863, John N. Goodwin became the first governor of this new territory. His headquarters were at Fort Whipple in the Prescott area. The Goodwin home is part of the

Sharlot Hall Museum in Prescott today. Sharlot Hall was an extraordinary woman. She is a rich part of Arizona history. In a way, she was a feminist because she did not believe that it was necessary for every woman to find her destiny through marriage.

As a state, Arizona has many assets, one of them being the weather. The Phoenix area enjoys warm and sunny winters, which are always followed by blazing hot summers. Millions of visitors winter in the Valley, fleeing from the cold winters in their home states. Residents often seek relief from the summer heat in the mountains. In the winter the mountains provide all of the winter sports. During WWII, airfields were built in Arizona. American and British pilots were trained at Falcon Field in Mesa. The weather was perfect and the climate is dry. Some of these men and their families returned after the war and formed a new generation of native Arizonans.

The State has a bright future and it has become a magnet for people from all over the country. Industry for the new millennium is well established here. The Indian and Hispanic influence remains strong in the architecture, the artifacts, and in the food.

The preceding paragraphs are not meant as a Chamber of Commerce commercial for Arizona, they are just my observations and thoughts.

Soon after I moved into the new house, I went to work. When I visited my sister in January 1977, I made the usual rounds of interviews looking for work. Sunshine does not come cheap. The nursing salaries at that time were very low. Although I never belonged to a union, my salary in Michigan benefited from union presence in that state. I also had the benefit of being a long term employee at Bon Secours Hospital. My salary decreased by about $8,000 per year when I moved to Arizona. I had not looked for a job for many years and I made a mistake; I accepted a position that offered the best salary for the first and only time in my life. In retrospect, a staff nurse position would have made the transition easier but the salary scale at that level was even lower.

In most hospitals there is a need to fill the night shift positions first. I knew that I could not cope with that; my inability to sleep in the daytime would have made that impossible. The position that I accepted was on the day shift. We live and we learn. It was not a happy choice and after two years I resigned. It was a mutual agreement for the employer and for me.

I had also been working part time at Desert Samaritan Hospital in Mesa. I liked the atmosphere and the people with whom I worked. I applied for a full-time position and was accepted as coordinator of the Critical Care Units. It was a good choice. "Desert Sam" was growing and continues to be a busy hospital in Mesa.

The early settlers in Mesa were of the Mormon faith. Two of these were John and Caroline Le Sueur. Originally their ancestors were from the Channel Island of Jersey. Although I am not related, or of the same faith of this family, I like the connection. The first hospital in Mesa was established in the Le Sueur home. This was enlarged and became known as the Southside Hospital. Progress demanded a larger facility to cope with the increasing population. Desert Samaritan Hospital evolved to fill this need. It opened in 1973. This new and modern hospital was built on land formerly known as the Dobson Ranch. The Dobson family were early settlers in Mesa.

I remembered seeing pictures of this new hospital in the desert when Bon Secours was converting to the "no nurse station" concept. This concept put the patient's chart and all of the patient supplies in a cupboard in the patient's room. The idea behind this philosophy being that the nurse would be closer to the patient. The nurses and the patients adapted but the medical staff nearly came unglued. This concept had not been used at "Desert Sam" but one nice feature was that all of the patient rooms are private.

The atmosphere at "Desert Sam" was a happy one. The medical staff was young and progressive. It was a busy hospital and the surrounding area was rapidly growing. The hospital was part of Samaritan Health Service. Good Samaritan, the largest and the oldest in the system, was in Phoenix. In the last 20 years this institution has continued to grow and serve the city of Mesa.

The Critical Care Units at that time consisted of three six-bed units. Two were for intensive care patients and the third was for coronary care patients. At Bon Secours the units were completely separate. The pressure for beds at Desert Sam made that impossible. For the nine years that I worked in the units, there never was a dull moment. Some of the original nurses at Southside Hospital transferred to Desert Samaritan.

My supervisor was from Michigan. She was a graduate of the University of Michigan. She was a delight to know and to work with. Alice was a worker and she had a great sense of humor. I have a favorite Alice story. One day she was called before the Dean of Women at U. of M. She was asked how many grandmothers she had. The then Alice Ashmore answered cheerfully "two." The Dean reminded Alice that according to her records six of them had died. She was Alice Carrigan by the time I met her.

Alice remembers coming into my office one day and seeing four sets of dentures on my desk. Another tooth story and another puzzle. The dentures were found in a cupboard but none had been reported as missing! Dentures are interesting. Owners are often careless with them. Ill people are especially vulnerable. Sometimes they lose them. Some they remove them to eat. Most often they are a problem if the patient vomits. Dentures are always removed before surgery. I can assure the reader that if dentures needed to be replaced, an upper and lower set was always requested. I often wondered if I should add a set of dentures to the budget each year.

Critical Care technology is expensive. The budget was always a challenge and a huge responsibility involving millions of dollars. Alice was creative. We struggled for hours. One late afternoon we took the paperwork with us to a restaurant so that we could eat and go over it one more time. The curious waitresses left us alone. I think that we worked until closing time.

I seemed to spend most of my time looking for beds and checking which patients were stable enough for transfer. I learned a new Doctor's order, "TIBN," transfer if bed needed. Working with the emergency room staff was crucial. They needed us and we needed them. The clerical staff in the Admitting office worked right along with us. The "unseen people" often go unrecognized in patient care, which is unfortunate. A close working relationship can help lighten the load of any busy day. I enjoyed the admitting clerks; they certainly did all that they could to help me.

The very worst part of my job was calling the nurses back to work or asking them to work overtime. It seemed that in Michigan the family units had been intact especially in the '50s and '60s. There was always a need for nurses. But in the '80s lives had changed. Single moms and divorce were now part of the picture. Some needed the overtime pay and some simply could not do it. Midnight shift was the most difficult to cover. By the time the units had expanded to 22 beds and the open-heart program was in place, it was even more complicated. We were calling the nurses back to work so often they got answering machines. I did not blame them. The '70s and especially the '80s brought a new kind of nurse, highly skilled and competitive.

Writing this story has reminded me that most of them had no concept of who had paved the way for them. The early nurses at Bon Secours Hospital and other institutions in this country forged ahead, embracing the new technology in its infancy. Once in a while it is good to remember, because the nurses of today will soon be looking back at themselves. Time marches on and however wonderful we think we are someone someday replaces all of us.

I needed to leave critical care nursing. An opening in the hospice department allowed me to transfer. December 7, 1987, I entered the final stage of a long career. East Valley Hospice was part of Desert Sam. I went out into the community for the first time in my career. I was making another change.

Some say that hospice care must be depressing work. Nothing is further from the truth. These patients know all about living and they can teach all of us about dying. Often they made me feel that I took them to the gates of Heaven.

I observed how much they appreciated their nurses' visits. The relationship between the hospice patient and the nurse is unique. It was the same in the early days of coronary care nursing, and hopefully still exists today. I observed so long ago that the patient was always closest to the nurse who cared for them when they were first admitted with chest pain. That was a scary time for the patient and the family. The patient looked to the nurse for relief and security.

For each one of us, nurse and patient, that was a special experience. Hospice nursing taught me a lot about illness, relationships, and the pressing need to value each person as they live. Eulogies at funerals are touching but as far as we know the deceased does not hear them.

Pain control for the cancer patient is as much a specialty as any high priced piece of equipment in the critical care unit. Dying of cancer is not a bed of roses but most of the pain can be controlled. I shudder every time I read of another patient desperate enough to seek relief from the Dr. Deaths of this world. Pain control takes skill and education. That means listening to the patient and teaching every family member or caregiver. Nurses and physicians also need to understand the use of narcotics and pain control.

Often patients are fearful that they will become drug addicts. They need to be taught that they are not seeking some kind of a high, but rather narcotics for them are like an antibiotic for an infection. The older generation often believe that the patient needs to eat to recover their "strength." It meant gently reassuring them that they were good caregivers but the patient with cancer feels worse if they force themselves to eat. We urged the patients to drink lots of water; up to eight glasses each day. That is not easy for them but it is important because narcotics are constipating.

An experienced hospice nurse is an asset to a physician as regards maintaining the patient on an adequate narcotic dose for pain control. Every once in a while I would run into a physician who feared that the patient would be overdosed or that prescribing such a dose would be violating the law. It required tact and persuasion and sometimes persistence.

I was amazed at how well the families adapted to the role of caregiver. At first some of them made it clear to me that the patient must not die at home. When questioned about what they imagined the dying process to be they gave all kinds of descriptions. Fear was the biggest stumbling block. With gentle guidance, and perhaps an extra visit or two, most of the patients died at home. The families were grateful and so were the patients. I do not know too many people that want to die in a hospital or a nursing home. Most of us dread it. Home is where the heart is.

Family pets grieve, too. A hospice nurse cares for the whole family. I met and enjoyed some wonderful pets. One deserves special mention. This was a parrot. The patient needed to have a urinary catheter inserted into his bladder. The parrot had free reign of the house and he was very protective of the family. His cage was alongside the bed. Memory may deceive me here but this pet sat on the side rail of the bed with an eye on me that was not encouraging. Catherization is not pleasant for any patient and certainly any nurse would want to minimize the discomfort for the patient. However under the glaring scrutiny of this parrot I do admit to praying that this would be a textbook procedure for all of us. This poor parrot grieved so deeply that by the time the patient died it had lost all of its feathers. Believe me, I nearly lost mine when I saw those eyes upon me.

The only difficult part of hospice work for me was being called out at night. We rotated on-call duty. Sometimes that involved being called out two or three times a night. The hard part was that one most often had to work the next day. By the end of two days like that, I was not ready to bet on surviving myself.

I truly enjoyed the work, the patients and their families. Those with no religious faith seemed to have a harder time but others were accepting that their earthly lives were coming to an end. For the most part I cared for senior citizens and they were like most of their generation, durable, honest, and grateful for any help given to them.

All of them helped me to conclude 48 years of nursing which was the choice I made as a little girl. I have walked away from a dream fulfilled to a retirement that is rich in new experiences and filled with wonderful friends.

CHAPTER FIFTEEN

Pets Who Have Owned Me

Of this I am certain: I have had the most wonderful pets and I have loved every one of them. Peter was the first one and I only know him from a photograph. I think he preceded me as a family member. He probably sensed the family tension when my parents tried to cope with this screaming infant. I bet he got his food and his tummy was full. In the first chapter, I described my parents' futile attempts to find a formula that satisfied me. It is a miracle that I survived but that is the peril of being the first born. My mother told me that Peter became my protector and sat by my high chair for hours. Question: Why was I in the high chair for hours? Too late for an answer now, Mom is in Heaven.

The next pet and the first I remember was a cat named Ginger. She got run over by a car and one of her legs was broken. I can recall nothing else, but I can see her in my memory.

I suppose the next big event was my baby sister. We moved to a new house after she was born. Houses have names in Jersey. Ours was called "Cappa White." It is the name of the village in Tipperary where my maternal grandmother was born. She was raised in England from the age of three months and I doubt that she ever returned to Ireland. By the oddest coincidence there is an Irish lady at church I currently attend, St. Timothy's Catholic Community, who comes from the next village to Cappa White. The owner who bought the house from us in 1956 never changed the name. Every time we go back to Jersey we take a sentimental look at it. It was the only home in Jersey that my sister ever knew and she has deep feelings for it.

During the Occupation I developed Hepatitis. I was ill for several months. No medicines were available during Occupation days, I simply was treated with bed rest. It is an exhausting illness at the best of times.I neither had the strength or the motivation to get going as I recovered. Dr. Mortimer Evans found a dog, Dusty, for me. This was to encourage me to become active again. Dusty knew he was mine for a purpose and he was the dearest companion. He was a Dandie Dinmont, a Scottish Terrier of the most aristocratic birth. He was a grey color. He had a brother who was named Rusty who was a redhead. We met him once. Of course I thought that Dusty was cuter!

Finding food for pets was no small task. We had a neighbor who worked at the abattoirs (slaughterhouse). He used to bring cow udders home and my mother cooked these for Dusty (I feel nauseous writing this). Dusty hated cats but that was his only fault. I believe that he must have contracted Nephritis (kidney disease) because he began to swell and had bloody urine. The vet was called and took him away. I wonder now what he used to put him down. Veterinary drugs must have been as scarce as any other medicines during the Occupation. What still hurts as I remember Dusty is the memory of him struggling up the stairs to be with me the night before he died. He was so ill and so faithful to me. Dusty, I love you to this day. You were my medicine and my friend.

Later in the Occupation, a friend of ours who was a housekeeper changed jobs because the elderly lady whose home she cared for died. By the strangest of coincidences, our friend was the aunt to the gentleman that bought Cappa White. We called her Auntie Addie. She had a cat and we gladly took him. His name was Paddy. He was a handsome boy, grey striped, and very easy going. Anne used to dress him in her doll's clothes and he would lie in her doll's pram for hours. He would get up and run around still wearing the clothes. Food for him was easier. There is a tiny shellfish in Jersey called a limpet. My mother cooked these for him. The smell of these limpets cooking was enough to make one want to move out of the house. Our next-door neighbor who evacuated to England with her husband in 1940 returned as a widow. Her husband had been killed in an air raid in England. There was a large fishpond in her garden. She filled it with goldfish. Paddy ate every one of them. She gave up eventually and planted flowers in the pond.

After the war, my mother bought cod for him. She told me that she had him put down because when she was a widow, his food became too expensive. I was in the United States at the time and I cannot even today bear to think of this.

No more pets until I bought Beau in 1971. He came from a lovely family in Farmington, Michigan. Their young daughter brought him back to Michigan in a shoebox from Sausilito, California. Her grandmother lived there and she raised poodles. Beau was a lovely apricot color. The family told me that a young couple had seen him but he growled at them. He was meant to be mine. When he died, 12 years later, I wrote to this family and told them how much happiness Beau had given me.

When I bought him, they gave me written instructions and hints about his habits, etc. This included the fact that he was used to sleeping in the bathroom. Well, I tried the first night, but he was in my bed before me. We both thought that was exactly the right place for him. He always had trouble with his stomach. He finally haemorrhaged and my vet, Dr. Beech, had to put him down. He was a dear dog and part of my Michigan and Arizona life. Beau translated from the French means beautiful, fine and handsome. Beau was all of these inside and out. For his American Kennel Association name, I chose the Duke of Normandy. A Duke of Normandy ruled Jersey at the end of the first millennium.

Next came Darcy, the cat of the century. What a character! Gorgeous and temperamental with everyone but me. She was a calico cat. Dr. Beech told me that Beau was lonely and that he advised me to get a cat as a companion for him. Beau missed my mother. At first I took him to her every day before I went to work, but when I moved to Mesa, that was no longer practical. Darcy was a stray. The family who rescued her had a Doberman. Darcy, a tiny little kitten, had terrorized this big dog. They were happy to send her to a good home.

I told my friend Eleanor Darcy Peterson in Michigan that I would name my cat after her. She always told me that none of her nieces or nephew had named their children Darcy and this disappointed her. It was perfect for my cat and Eleanor was my first visitor in Tempe. Darcy was not a bit interested in the origin of her name. She ignored Eleanor. For the 12 years that I had her she only accepted me.

Beau was upset for three days when I first brought her home. We both learned to live with this haughty cat. She was a good girl at heart; she only bit my friends. Darcy had big yellow eyes. She was longhaired and fluffy. Her markings were white, black, and orange. Her back legs looked like pantaloons and she flounced around the house. The black color marked her face like a mask and she looked like a bandit. When my mother came to visit, she always brought cake for her tea. Darcy knew this and she considered the crumbs from the cakes to be her treat. Darcy was a presence in the house. She walked around with her nose in the air, but she was no trouble. When I moved to the single-family home, she had the laundry room for her food and litter box. When it pleased her, she let me brush her. She had thick fur, so it was not a two-minute job. She had her special moments with me. She slept on my bed on the pillow and she would purr and stroke my face with her paw. She had a great personality. She was not calm when she went to the vet. She had to be muzzled before Dr. Beech could examine her. He said once after the struggle was over that she was a real bitch. He also told me that beautiful cats often have difficult personalities. I choose to remember her as the original "Spice" girl.

I decided that I wanted another dog. Several people told me that I was foolish. I was determined, however, and the house was plenty big enough. I bought another poodle. At least I thought I had another poodle. I saw an ad in the paper. Anne and I went to see the puppy. She came from a breeder and she had all of the papers. When we arrived, there were two puppies and we were told that they were brother and sister. The smaller one was the female. She was very active and was pushing the other puppy all over the room. Her color was white and she had a beautiful face with sparkling black eyes. I was ripe for a dog and I bought her. She had very tiny ears and the owners assured me that they would grow. I took her to Dr. Beech the next day for a check up. He said, "Sheila, this is not a poodle. If she is, she is a throw back." Her front legs were short and she had the most awkward looking long back legs. She never was able to roll over on her back. I had a list of French names ready for her, but none of them suited this little bundle of energy. I remarked to Anne that she was a tough little thing and from that moment on she was Tuffy. She was a funny looking dog with the sweetest personality and a beautiful face. She was no push over, however, and she was determined to do whatever she wanted. From the first moment Darcy set eyes on Tuffy, she hated her. She hissed at her for eight days. Beau was fine and he helped me endure the tension. Darcy was a real pain. They never reconciled but that never bothered Tuffy. Dr. Beech always called her the girl from Globe. Globe is a mining town up in the mountains. I guess one might say that Tuffy was a mountain girl. She was a little rough around the edges. Soon after I had her, I found her eating her feces. I was horrified and she had her mouth cleaned until it shone. I had no idea that some dogs do this. I had my work cut out, but I turned her into a princess. My mother thought I was wrong to get another dog. Tuffy took care of that. She won Grandma over in a very short time. They were inseparable. Tuffy did not need legs; she was always curled up on my mother's lap.

Tuffy always went to bed promptly at 7.30. She would walk half way down the hall toward the bedroom, look back at me for the okay, and that was the end of Tuffy until the morning. We were now three in the bed. Darcy waited until the dogs were asleep before joining us. Beau was coming to the end of his life. I knew it and dreaded the inevitable. Dr. Beech put him down. It was the week that President Regan was shot.

The following September, I brought Chip home. I bought him from a nice young lady. No more kennel dogs for me. Chip was a toy poodle and his color was dark chocolate. It was difficult to see his brown eyes. He was a little sweetheart. I tried the same routine because supposedly he also slept in the kitchen. That did not work and so we all slept together. I used to sleep wherever I could find a spot to fit in the bed.

Darcy liked and approved of Chip. That was a relief. Tuffy was cool. In fact, Tuffy and Chip would race around the house and nearly trip me up. On one occasion I took the dogs up to Prescott, in the mountains of Arizona, for a couple of days. My neighbor agreed to look in on Darcy. She got into the house all right, but Darcy barred the door and she had to call her husband to rescue her. When we returned, Darcy was not happy. She got up on her haunches and sniffed both of the dogs. I suppose she was curious as to where they had been. I never left her alone again.

Darcy became ill and it was obvious that it was serious. Once more Dr. Beech took care of her. She fought him right until the end. Tuffy and Chip moved to this present house with me. They were so good and adjusted very well. We had several more trips to Prescott and I really wanted to retire up there. Prescott is a small town with lots of history. Now, like every place in Arizona, it is growing at a rapid pace. When the economy was in a downturn in California, there was a significant number of Californians who moved to Prescott. With that, the price of real estate sky rocketed and that ended my retirement plans.

After we lived in this house for six months, Tuffy developed cancer in her nasal sinuses. Once more Dr. Beech put another of my pets down. Every one of the veterinary staff loved the "girl from Globe." She had a way of making herself so lovable. Chip was a wreck; he lost weight and was terrified of being left alone in the house. He was always tightly attached to me. He had to be with me and he never let me out of his sight. In May 1995, when Anne and I went back to Jersey to celebrate 50 years of freedom, Dedra, one of Dr. Beech's staff, came to care for him. Neither Chip nor I could have survived if I had boarded him. Of course, I called from Europe to check on him. Chip was a routine kind of guy and he kept me in line. He was totally dependent on me. For the last three years of his life I never left him and I have absolutely no regrets. He became deaf and the last week of his life totally blind. He was terrified he could no longer see or hear me. I took him into see Dr. Beech and he put Chip down.

Tuffy and Chip were cremated and I had them put in the same container. They are under my bed and that is where they belong in their home. If the world thinks that I am over the top on this, I really do not care. They were my family and I cared for them very well. They were always happy to see me and all they wanted was room and board and love.

A word about the family vet. Even that is threatened now with large vet offices. Something on the order of managed care. Well, I wanted a relationship with a vet I knew and trusted. It was like a family affair and my pets were always treated with care and compassion. I certainly am not suggesting that these new pet clinics are lacking in care or compassion. I used them in emergency situations with Tuffy. They were kind and efficient. I often thought, sitting in the office waiting room, how owners resemble their pets. If looked like mine that's okay too.

I will not replace Chip because a commitment to a pet is one that I do not feel would be right at my age. I need the freedom and I have the wonderful memories. It has been quite painful to write this chapter. They were a special part of my life and I loved every one of them.

Pet care has made enormous progress. All of mine had their teeth cleaned once year and I struggled with the doggie toothbrush and paste on a daily basis. Except for Darcy, she was not about to open her mouth for anyone. The dogs went to be groomed on a monthly basis so it can be expensive. Dr. Beech was my family vet for over 20 years. I appreciated him and his staff very much. When my pets needed care they always gave me an appointment. We became good friends over the years.

CHAPTER SIXTEEN

Retirement
New Life - New Opportunities

I truly looked forward to retirement. I never imagined how well it would all work out. It is not like a vacation; for me it is a new life. From the very first day, I have woken up each morning with a delicious feeling of freedom. There never is a bad day when one is healthy, and I am blessed in that respect. It must be the Jersey genes. I did have hyperthyroidism in the '60s. I was treated successfully with radioactive iodine, but even that did not slow me down. On the contrary, I seem to have more energy than ever. Other than the usual things like a hysterectomy (the best operation ever performed, in my opinion), I have cruised through life with great good health. I clearly understand how fortunate I am in that respect.

I had no definite plans. I just sensed that somehow everything would work out. I joined an aerobics group, visited friends in Michigan and Massachusetts, and just kept busy. I worked for Hospice on a part-time basis until I moved in July 1993. I learned very quickly retirement days pass twice as fast as workdays. I believe 48 years as a nurse was enough. What I did not anticipate was just how much my life would change. I had no sooner moved than my car developed problems. As a hospice nurse, it was not unusual to put a thousand miles a month on the car. I decided to buy another Honda. I started out with a new house and a new car. Things were moving right along. I spent a lot of energy and time on my house.

In the fall of '93, I reconnected with the Sisters of Bon Secours. Sister Anna Mae Crane moved to Arizona. We had one day to find her a house, and we found one! That was a high-pressure day if ever there was one. Anna Mae worked in Phoenix for three years. She became one of the family, and we had the pleasure of her company for all of the holidays. Sister Anne Lutz, Sister Rita Thomas, and Sister Anne Marie Mack, all visited during those years. We had a great reunion. My nieces and nephew still miss Anna Mae and her dogs.

Anna Mae is a marvellous cook, so we went back and forth to one another's homes for meals. We enjoyed lots of good times together. Lots of laughter and reminisces about the good old days at Bon Secours Hospital in Grosse Pointe, Michigan.

Classmates from England visited. When Ida (classmate from midwifery) came in 1994, I had my first ever visit to Disneyland. It is true that something magical happens when one walks through the gates. We had a happy visit. I got stuck in one of the rides with Anne, and we thought that we would never extricate ourselves. Much to the annoyance of the man in charge of the ride, we could not stop laughing. Ida was on the sidelines urging us on, so that made us laugh all the harder. Ida and Anne decided to go into the Star Wars movie and I tagged along. I kept my eyes closed all through the whole show. No guts. Ida and Anne said that it was great. When I lived in Michigan, Joan Kettel and I went to see the movie "Jaws." I kept my eyes closed through the entire movie. I simply could not watch it. No offence to Steven Spielberg.

GOLDEN ANNIVERSARY 1995

Anne and I planned to be in Jersey for the celebrations of the 50th anniversary of our Liberation: May 9, 1995. My poodle, Chip, was now an only dog, and I dreaded leaving him. We planned on being away for a month. My vet, Dr. Beech and staff said they would take care of Chip. Dedra Warwick, a former nurse who worked for Dr. Beech, lived at my house for the entire time. It was such a relief for me. Walking out of the house was very difficult because I knew that Chip knew that I was leaving. I admit I called from Europe to check on his survival.

After months of planning and anticipation, we boarded a plane at Sky Harbor Airport in Phoenix for Los Angeles. Our Virgin Atlantic flight did not depart for London until 7 p.m. We checked our bags in at 1 p.m., and we were surprised that security procedure was so tight. The date was April 19, 1995. Finally it was time to board the aircraft. The passengers seemed to be as anxious as we were to get started, particularly those with young children. Suddenly the boarding stopped. I am not clear on the details, but apparently a bag had been passed to a passenger in the line. The result was that the baggage hold was emptied and the plane was searched. This was not a reassuring start to the flight.

The plane was crowded and it was not a comfortable flight. A huge man in the seat in front of me spilled over into my space. I could hardly move my legs for the entire flight.

We landed in London and took the transport to our hotel. Anne bought a paper and we were horrified to read of the Oklahoma bombing. The hotel turned out to be a dump. We made several phone calls, and after several refusals were lucky to find accommodation at the Marriot in Duke Street in London. We looked out of our hotel window and we saw the American Embassy. The building had altered from the charming old Victorian house. It was now a rather forbidding concrete building. Much more significantly to me, I was back at the exact location that I had started from on my American journey in 1952. I applied for my visa to enter the United States at that very Embassy!

The stay at the Marriot was wonderful. Two days later I returned to the London Hospital for my 50th reunion with my classmates. The actual reunion date was October 1995, but my friends advanced the celebration to coincide with my visit to England. Anyone who has had a reunion with friends from their student days knows what an incredible experience it is and ours was no less wonderful. No one in 1945 could have predicted that I would spend most of my life living and working in the United States.

The exterior of the London Hospital looked the same as I exited from the familiar Whitechapel underground station. Walking in the front entrance was an emotional experience; I remembered the first time so well. Then came the shock. The porters were gone from where I expected to find them. In their place was a bank. The white tile walls had vanished too. They had been replaced, and all along the walls hung paintings just as one so often sees in an American hospital.

The Luckes Nursing Residence was another shock to me. The steps looked as though they had not been cleaned since the day Pauline's father picked us up in 1949! Some of my classmates stayed in the Luckes for the reunion. They described how much the old home had changed, and it was not for the better. We had changed too, but the years had been kinder to us. I prefer the old memories.

We attended the Annual League Day and luncheon (London Hospital for Nurses). League Day is a combination of business meetings and lectures. The day concluded with a church service in a wonderful old church close to the hospital named St.Dunstans. Cardinal Basil Hume of England gave the homily. He told us that he felt close to the London Hospital nurses because his father had been a London Hospital doctor.

As we filed out he shook our hands. I told him that I was from America. He raised his hands in the air and exclaimed in a loud voice, "From America!" It was a special moment for me as a Catholic.

We planned to be in Jersey for the anniversary of our Liberation: May 9, 1995. After two weeks in England visiting with Pauline and Ida, Anne and I set foot on Jersey soil. The weather was glorious just as it had been on May 9, 1945. Only now, we were American citizens. The official ceremonies took place opposite the house where we had been born as Channel Islanders and as British subjects. We spoke about it in a light-hearted manner. It was, however, a significant experience for both of us.

THE AMERICAN POWs
JERSEY, AUGUST 1944-1945

In 1994, I received a book from Gillian Willis (she had been my air raid companion) titled "Lest We Forget" by Roy Thomas. In it I read of the true stories of the young Jersey men who had escaped from Jersey to France during the Occupation. These escapes were fraught with danger and attempted under the most hazardous conditions. Some were successful, some were recaptured, and others drowned. The stories are touching and inspiring. They remind us once more of how precious freedom is and how love of country makes men and women go to desperate lengths.

Two of the stories included by Mr. Thomas involved American officers Ed Clark and George Haas. They were captured in Normandy in 1994 in the area close to St. Malo. The Germans transported them to Jersey in August 1944, along with several other American soldiers, some of whom were wounded. At that point in the battle, there was no way they could be sent through the lines to Germany. Ed and George made a successful escape to France from the prison camp in Jersey in January 1945. The stories of their escape are incredible. Both of these men credit the courage of the Jersey families who risked their lives to hide them and help them escape. In fact, there is a plaque in Jersey at the site of their escape to commemorate them for all time. Once more I get ahead of myself.

After reading the book I knew that I had to find these men. I remembered their escape. The Germans issued a proclamation warning   Jersey people if they assisted the Americans the penalty was death. They were not fooling. Later we learned the escape route the POWs took brought them close to our house.

Fifty years later in Arizona my search began, and I thought at first I was looking for just two men. I contacted Bruce Willing who was in charge of all the anniversary celebrations in Jersey. I had read that the Americans were to be honored at a special event January 19, 1995, the anniversary of the date that they made their escape to France in 1944. They escaped from the camp January 8 and were in hiding in the fields, and eventually in a haystack, until the weather conditions made it possible for them to leave. That particular winter was exceptionally cold. In fact, the weather was dreadful with gales, and it snowed, which was unusual for Jersey. Bruce was able to give me their addresses and telephone numbers. Ed lived in Texas and George in New York.

I called Ed Clark and he was really surprised. He came to Arizona to visit Anne and I the following weekend. It was quite a moment when we met Ed at the airport. The camp where the Americans were imprisoned was not far from our home although we had no contact with them. Anne remembers seeing some of them walking to a hotel with a cart where they picked up their soup rations. Cabbage soup was the main dish. She and some other children would help them push the cart up the hill. They were accompanied by armed German guards who did not chase the children away.

At school our class was encouraged to send some food to these men. Everyone wanted to help the Americans. My mother made some cookies out of what little we had, and so we sent those. They must have tasted terrible. My mother was a good cook but times were hard and food and ingredients were down to little or nothing.

Back to 1994. Ed told me to contact Colonel Bob Dwan who lives in Tucson, Arizona. Colonel Dwan is a retired career officer, graduate of Westpoint and a veteran of the Normandy campaign, whose hobby is researching WWII and assisting authors in identifying details for their stories. Ed told me that Colonel Dwan would help me locate some of the other POWs. I called Colonel

Dwan and, as promised, the search began. It was all consuming and great fun. Bob Dwan literally found them dead or alive. It took several months. Eventually I had contacted a dozen or so of these men. They all remembered their captivity in this unknown part of the world to most Americans, the Channel Island of Jersey. A group of them decided to return to Jersey and take part in the anniversary celebrations.

Bruce Willing and I had a regular correspondence going, interspersed with many phone calls. One of my acquired American characteristics is using the phone often and effectively!

When we were liberated the American prisoners were also freed. It took some days for the American authorities to get them out of the Island, so they were temporarily housed at the Omarroo Hotel at Havre des Pas in Jersey. For the anniversary trip, I was able to arrange accommodations for them at the Ommaroo. When they arrived in Jersey, most of them were meeting one another for the first time in 50 years.

Eight of the American former POWs made the trip. They were Custer Quick (Wyoming), Newell Younggren (Arizona), Warren Sidney (New Jersey), Armand Du Bois (Massachusetts), Bob Hanson (South Dakota), and Joe Russomano (New Jersey). Ed Clark is a Texan through and through. George Haas is from New York. George and Ed have made several return visits to Jersey over the years. Newell Younggren has also visited Jersey with his grandsons.

Newell was a member of the American military government. The Germans made a raid in Granville, Normandy March 1945. Newell was captured as he slept in a hotel. He was wearing new pajamas that he had just received from his mother in the States. The Germans were in a rush and captured Newell in his pajamas, which became his prison garb. Newell donated the pajamas to the Jersey museum some years later, where they are currently on display. All of these men have wonderful stories and they are absolutely part of the Greatest Generation.

Joe Russomano died in July 1998. He was a real character. He kept separating himself from the group and I would have to go looking for him. I decided then and there that being a tour guide was not for me.

All of us enjoyed the celebrations. The Jersey people gave the men a real Jersey welcome. We were at one event in the beautiful Howard Davis Park in Jersey. A lady approached me and told me that she had taught me at Mandalay School. We figured out the year was 1933 and I was six years old. Which goes to show that I have not changed much (just kidding of course). I did not remember her specifically, but I do remember someone trying to teach me to sew. We, or rather the teacher, did most of the sewing and the end result was a clothes bag which went over a clothes hanger. My mother saved it. I have it here in Arizona. I was so stunned that I neglected to ask her name. When I returned to Arizona, I wrote to the Jersey Weekly Post and was able to trace her. She is Mrs. D'Orleans. Life is full of wonderful surprises.

After a stop in Guernsey to visit lifelong friends Dennis and Fay Le Sueur, Anne and I returned to Arizona with so many memories and hundreds of photographs! Home at last, Chip and I were both happy to be reunited.

In the fall, Anne saw an ad in the Mesa Tribune about New Frontiers for Learning in Retirement at Mesa Community College. They were advertising for an Open House. We decided to go and check it out. We walked in and proceeded to visit all of the booths. One sign read "World War II Coffee and Conversations." We approached the facilitator, Millicent Salm, who asked us where we came from. We replied, "From Jersey in the Channel Islands." Millicent exclaimed that her best friends lived there. We replied, "not New Jersey," thinking, as most Americans do, that we meant New Jersey. She insisted that she meant our Jersey. We signed up for Millicent's class and became members of New Frontiers Learning in Retirement.

That single moment started me on a journey. It continues even to this day. I hope it goes on forever. My retirement adventure had begun and it is moving full steam ahead.

CHAPTER SEVENTEEN

New Frontiers For Learning In Retirement

New Frontiers for Learning in Retirement is a peer-led group of senior learners who facilitate classes for one another in the community college setting. Mesa Community College in Mesa, Arizona, is our home base. Classes are held at the many campuses of the college. Mesa Community College is part of the Maricopa Community College District, the largest in the country. As long as I have lived in Arizona (over 20 years), I have heard about the great atmosphere on the campus. I truly enjoy my association with this school.

The focus is based on the fact learning is a life-long process. Classes are non-credit; there are no tests and no final exams. There is a flat fee that entitles the member to attend any classes offered throughout the year. Such a deal is irresistible. The curriculum is as varied as the facilitators who choose them. Usually the variety is such that something can be found to interest everyone. Topics vary from theater, politics, computers, history, language, art, photography, Scottish country dancing, and genealogy – just a huge variety!

This is where I found myself in September of 1995. Soon after I joined, I received notice of a business meeting. I believe at that time they nominated officers for the coming year. I went to the meeting out of curiosity, to check out this group of people, not entirely sure that I wanted to belong. I had paid my dues so I definitely thought I needed to be at the meeting, see what I'd gotten myself into. About the time I thought the meeting was winding down, I got up to leave, but I was confronted before I could leave and was asked what committee I would like to serve on. My instant reply was "None of them." There was no leaving; I was stuck. I had three choices: Curriculum (I said to myself, "Teachers. No thanks"), Finance (I am no star with my checkbook, perhaps I would be humiliated), so I settled for the third choice which was Membership. I like people and did not see too many hurdles there. It was a good choice. Four years later, I am still on the Membership committee, and also on the Curriculum committee.

The fact is, this organization was barely eighteen months old when I joined. I certainly do not want to scare new members off by implying there are strong-arm tactics used to get members on a committee. I, however, strongly recommend new members to serve on committees. It is a great way to learn about the organization and to make new friends.

In January 1996 we were able to recruit enough new members to claim 65 total memberships. Spring of 2000 it is approaching 400! We are a thriving organization, and with growth the curriculum is also broadening. Computer classes are always full.

At the initial meeting, I learned as a member I would be strongly advised to function as a facilitator. I made up my mind to avoid this at all costs. I certainly did not want to do anything with nursing, and I was at a complete loss as to what I could do.

The work on the Membership committee was lively and interesting. It was decided that we should look for additional social activities out of the classroom setting. Several proposals were considered and adopted. I volunteered to arrange for a group to attend the "Coffee Classics" concerts series offered by the Phoenix Symphony in Phoenix. These are offered on selected Friday mornings at 11 a.m. These concerts are very popular and always full. A distinguishing feature is all the grey-haired folks who don't drive at night!

We started with one concert. Fortunately, this activity has proven to be very popular and each year attendance has grown. We have lunch downtown after the concert and it makes for a pleasant event.

I coordinated this for three years. I stepped down for two reasons: First, I believe that it is a mistake for an individual to stay in any position too long. As our membership grows, new members should be encouraged to participate and new ideas are always healthy and refreshing. No one is indispensable, and retirement needs to be flexible. The second reason being that I am writing this story, and I found out early on that this is a full-time adventure. The symphony tradition has been established, which is the important point to remember. I'm pleased to have helped get it started and organized.

One of the most popular groups in New Frontiers is the Desert Rats. It is a large enthusiastic group of adventurers who explore the desert southwest. This is a learning activity, and members research the areas to be explored and share the information along the way. It does not appeal to me, but the Rats are believers. They go on extended trips all over the Southwest. Their leader, Dick Schifler, is known as the King Rat.

I continued to be concerned with what in the world I could do to facilitate a class. That all changed for me Memorial Day 1997, the day I became aware of Alexis de Tocqueville.

CHAPTER EIGHTEEN

Alexis de Tocqueville

Hippolyte had a career in the military. Edouard was destined to become a cultured and conservative seigneur and head of the family. The present members of the Tocqueville family are directly descended from Edouard.

Alexis and his brothers were educated in the aristocratic tradition of the day. They were entrusted to the care of the family priest who helped form their characters. He taught them right from wrong and introduced them to their Catholic faith. His name was Abbe Le Sueur and he is described as a venerable and kindly man. Alexis loved this gentle priest.

When I read the name of the priest my eyes flew wide open. I knew that the name Le Sueur was of Norman origin. The name first appears in Jersey around the 1300s. Refugees from Normandy who fled from Normandy for political or religious reasons introduced the name to the Island. Of noble origin, it became one of the names in Jersey.

Jersey was originally part of the Duchy of Normandy. History has placed the island into a unique position. It is located just a few miles off the coast of Normandy and yet it is attached to the English crown. This dates back to the Battle of Hastings in 1066. Relationships with France have existed for centuries. Originally part of the landmass of what is now France, it became separated during the ice age. There have been many wars over time.

The Boston Tea Party and the War of American Independence precipitated one such crisis. In 1778 France made a military alliance with the American rebels. Jersey's trade with the Colonies was threatened and its close proximity to France difficult on both sides of the Atlantic. England's punishment for the Alliance was to encourage Jersey privateers to plunder French shipping. Jersey and Guernsey and their pirating of French shipping were a serious problem for the French government. The frustration precipitated the invasion of Jersey in 1781. The French force invaded the Island and was soundly defeated in the Battle of Jersey. After the war ended the privateers returned to their normal commercial work. Much to the relief of all parties concerned.

Controversies arise over fishing rights but in general wiser heads prevail and the modern relationships are cordial. Channel Islanders are by nature independent, protective of their heritage, which they proclaim with pride. Neither French nor English the islands have been influenced by both cultures for centuries. Many of the laws in Jersey are based on the Norman tradition and continue until this day. The exception being criminal law which is similar to that of Britain.

There were other reasons why I began to feel so connected to Alexis de Tocqueville. My great grandmother Sophie Le Brun was born in 1831. She married Charles Le Sueur my great grandfather. One of their daughters, sister to my grandfather was Helena Jane Le Sueur. I knew her very well. She died while I was a student nurse in London. If only I could talk with her today. I feel a real affection for Sophie. If only, I tell myself, I could stop in her home for a cup of tea. The questions I would have. Too bad we are so unaware and uninterested of our family history in our youth. The third startling discovery, which I learned, was that an Alderney cow was on board the sailing ship that Tocqueville and his companion sailed in from Cherbourg to New York in 1831. Live provisions were needed for the long journey. Alderney is the most northerly of the Channel Islands.

The official reason for their journey to America was to study the new American penal system and report back to the French government. The French political system had failed to stabilize after the revolution. Alexis de Tocqueville was raised in the ultra conservative tradition. He had studied law and practiced his profession as a magistrate in Paris where he met another young magistrate Gustav de Beaumont. A friendship was formed that was to last a lifetime.

In July 1830 the French government was in chaos. The event known as the July Revolution saw the Bourbon King, Charles X, forced to abdicate and flee the country. Citizen King Louis Phillipe of Orleans seized power and was crowned. The Tocqueville family, loyal to the Bourbons, left the court and returned to their chateau in Normandy. Alexis and his friend Gustav were in Paris and survived the uprising. Later they were forced to sign allegiance to this new regime and both found this contrary to their beliefs.   He was a thinker and an observer, which affected his political ideas. This meant that his views were different from his traditions and his family. He questioned his faith.   Abbe' Le Sueur feared that this might happen. Alexis sincerely wished to be of service to his country but the Orleans regime would not be where he wished to serve. His liberal thoughts were just beginning to surface. He realized that he needed time away from the country. His friend Gustav de Beaumont had similar thoughts although he was more of a dreamer than Tocqueville who wanted action. They formulated a plan to visit America.

They obtained permission to go on a mission for the French government to study and report on the reforms in the American penal system. Tocqueville had heard and was curious to learn more of this new Republican form of government which he feared would replace the monarchy. Permission was given for the young magistrates to make the journey and to remain in America for nine months. The government refused to finance the mission. Family members and friends were able to provide financial assistance for the young friends. They sailed on the Harve from Cherbourg on April 2 1830. They disembarked in Newport, Rhode Island May 9, 1830.

The original port of arrival was New York but the live provisions, which Tocqueville described as Noahs Ark, were now gone. The Captain either fed them too well during the journey or he miscalculated the needs of the passengers and crew. Presumably the Alderney cow had not survived the journey. Alexis de Tocqueville and Gustav de Beaumont eagerly went ashore and explored Newport.They found a clean and attractive town with small houses which they described as "chicken coops." The next morning, their bags were checked at the customs and they had to swear that they had not brought any dutiable goods into the country. They were unable discern any easily identifiable racial characteristics in the facial features of the Americans They described the Americans as a mixture of all nations. They had been told that the women in Newport were beautiful but in this very short visit they described them as "extraordinarily ugly." Their most subtle observation was that they found this race to be entirely "commercial." They based this opinion in the fact that in the small city of Newport they found four or five banks. What they had discovered was DEMOCRACY!

The C-SPAN series retraced the journey of these young friends over a ten-month period. I began to learn and understand Democracy. When he returned to France, Tocqueville completed his mission and reported on the American penal system to the French Government. In 1834 he retired to the Chateau in Normandy and wrote his masterpiece, "Democracy in America." This book has never been out of print.

The friends sailed on a steamship from Newport and arrived in New York May 12 1831. Tocqueville was 25 years old. One hundred and twenty one years later, I sailed into New York on the Queen Elizabeth. I was 25 years old. It was November 26, 1952, and it was Thanksgiving eve. I am writing this Chapter on November 26, 1999, 47 years after the day I arrived in New York.

As I read the book, Tocqueville in America by George Wilson Pierson I knew that for me there was no turning back. I read it from cover to cover in five weeks. A true miracle for me. I have described my first impressions of arriving in New York in an earlier chapter. I was startled with the American energy and self-confidence. Beaumont writes to his mother that on there in New York they were overwhelmed with the courtesy and services extended to them.. They found that they had no need of the letters of introduction, which they had been given before leaving France.

The C-SPAN series followed the exact route of the adventure of the young French aristocrats. For me, it was like a guided tour. America opened up before my eyes. At each location I learned the history, saw wonderful views of the towns and countryside. Local citizens participated and described with pride the stories of their towns. I learned so much from them and felt the warmth that only the American personality can portray. I began to feel a real kinship with all of these people and how I wished that I could visit all of these incredible places in America.

I taped all of the programs. Best of all I was getting a picture of America. I knew that I wanted to share the excitement that I felt with my friends in New Frontiers for Learning at Mesa Community College. I could hardly keep up with what I was learning and feeling This was a grand experience for me. I also realized with a jolt that what I needed was to learn American history. It amazed me that I had lived so many years in this country and that I had missed so much. The fall semester was just around the corner and I signed up for a class on " The Federalist Papers." It was part of the curriculum offered in the fall semester by New Frontiers. I found it very difficult and I knew that before I could appreciate these writings I needed to start from the beginning. I signed up for History 103 with the regular students. It was summer school, so I went to class four days a week. For me it was a non credit class so that meant that I did not have to take the final exam. I found it much easier to listen when I did not have to worry about exams. I did take the take home tests each night. When I walked into the classroom one of the students asked me if I was the professor. I quickly reassured him.

Dr. John Ohl was the professor and I shall never forget him or the classes. He walked into the classroom and proceeded to move all of the desk furniture, overhead projector where he wanted them without saying a word or looking up. I thought to myself what have I done? Actually I did very well.

Dr. Ohl had just returned from Washington DC where he had been doing research for his third book. Flight delays meant that he had just arrived in town. Dr. Ohl made the history and the people who have shaped this nation come alive for me. The class took me up to the firing of the first gun in the Civil War. For the first time I got the concept of the States. The United States. When I moved to Arizona from Michigan I was surprised that I had to apply for another license to practice nursing. History 103 was just what I needed. It helped me learn about democracy.

A word about the young students in the class. They were exceptionally welcoming to me. When one of them asked me if I had the answer to one of the questions on the take home test I all but fell out of my desk. I appreciated them and they were easy to be with. There are lots of good young people in this country. Most of these students were balancing work with school. The greatest difficulty I had in preparing classes for our group was condensing all of this material into six sessions. I had great cooperation at Mesa. Community College. Lyn Hochstadter one of our members and a friend of mine supported me throughout. She is web master for our group. Before the classes she established a web page as part of the introduction.

The tapes that I had taken from the program needed to be edited. Once more I found the great enthusiasm from the video services at the college. Supposedly, I learned to edit them. It would be a gross exaggeration on my part to imply that! Ken Costello who graciously agreed to teach me did most of the work. One day he said to me "Sheila, this is not that difficult all you need is patience." I am forever grateful to Ken and it when it was all over he said that if necessary I could come back again. Ken is an expert and well respected among the college community.

I developed a close relationship with this department. During the series, C-SPAN held a contest. Nothing could me back I decided to enter it. The challenge was to say what I had learned about democracy from the series. The entries could be a piece of art (I was not able to draw so much as a box at Mandalay school) write a poem (Daffodils ruined that for) submit an audio tape or a video. I decided on a video. The making of that video became an epic of my lifetime. Ron Rangle was the key to my success. Another member of video services he coached me and I made the video. It was a real learning experience. When after what seemed to be many sessions Ron and Ken worked on it and produced my entry for the contest.

I shall never forget seeing it for the first time. I could not bear to look at it. I cringed. I was totally embarrassed. I certainly did not want anyone else to see it. I got over myself and sent it to C-SPAN.

I explained what I learned about democracy in three segments. They were Education, Free press-Free Speech and an Active Citizenry. Tocqueville described these as being the components for a successful Democracy. I drew on my experiences at the College for education, the Occupation years when I had no freedom or the privilege of the Vote. I hope that I can be forgive when I tell the reader that my video made me one of the fifty first place winners in the contest. I was seventy years old and for me that honor was as good as winning a gold medal in the Olympics. I told the world, called friends in Jersey. The prize was a 19-inch TV set. When the UPS lady delivered it she told the whole neighborhood. It was very exciting. Thank you, C-SPAN. This summer I had the thrill of visiting the C-SPAN network offices in Washington, DC. The journey continues and there are surprises around every corner.

CHAPTER NINETEEN

Democracy and Politics

DEMOCRACY

My journey into understanding how I became an American citizen was greatly enhanced by what I learned from Alexis de Tocqueville. His writings opened a door for which I had been searching a very long time. I truly wanted to understand democracy. I felt the freedom that living in this country afforded me and I heard others refer to it as unique. I wanted to know more. These are some of the ideas and conclusions that I have learned in my pursuit of the truth.

Democracy is a simple word with unbelievable depth. It is also tantalizing. When I embarked on this adventure I felt from the very beginning I was on a journey; I was powerless to resist. I liked the feeling so I just went with the flow. I had no control as the thoughts burst out of my mind like fireworks on the Fourth of July. If I am not working at the computer, I am thinking about the next sentence. I wake up in the night and I promise myself that I shall remember the words in the morning. Each day of this journey surprises me because each day there is another link in this chain of events. It is exciting; it is absolute wonderment for me.

When I stop to really think about democracy, its meaning is endless. My impression is that its strength is that it belongs to the people. Its weakness is that all people are flawed and too often the real meaning of democracy is not appreciated. That is freedom.

I believe that <u>freedom</u> is as vital to the human being as water, air, and food. It has a price and that is responsibility. It also takes work. Freedom never takes a holiday. It thrives on energy, teamwork, and enthusiasm.

The Constitution of the United States as I read it (I am only a learner in this respect) speaks for the individual and the inherent right of freedom for all of its citizens. One example is the VOTE that is the tool that allows the citizen to participate in Democracy. I know that this is impossible, but try to imagine if this privilege at the voting booth were revoked. The line at the polling booth would be endless. Tell Americans that they cannot do something and they will prove you a liar every time. Why, I ask myself, do some Americans not exercise this right? Is it because they know that they have the right not to vote? That is where it gets confusing. /Especially when we read about other countries that have never had either right. Tocqueville was an aristocrat in a country where the lower class had none of these rights yet he understood the privilege of the American system.

POLITICS

They are often frustrating but always interesting. The Occupation years convinced me that I never wanted to be lose my freedom again. Consequently, I have always kept an eye on the politics, especially in Europe. I claim no expertise, but I often wonder where all of the statesmen have gone. Early in this story I explained that I am registered as an Independent. Sometimes this makes me feel that I have less influence, but I hesitate to lose the freedom of choice that it gives me. I look for leadership, integrity, trust, strength, gentleness, and an individual who inspires others to be the best that they can be. Winston Churchill was all of that for me. Pauline, my friend from our student days in London, and her husband, Angus, took Anne and me to Winston Churchill's home Chartwell, England, for a visit in 1991. I stood in awe in his dining room; it is a long room with a large bay window overlooking the grounds. The dining room chairs were up holstered in an apple green colored chintz material. At least that is how I remember it. The room had an informal and welcoming atmosphere. I stood in awe as the guide described that a frequent dinner guest during WWII was General Eisenhower. To stand in the room where the leaders who guided the troops who brought us freedom May 9, 1945, was overpowering. My words are inadequate as I try to express my feelings 54 years later. Liberation Day will be with me forever.

Modern politics are rough and tumble, but they probably are reflection of our times. For the past 10 months, I have learned the history of the 41 Presidents of the United States. C-SPAN is closing the century with an incredible gift to the nation. For 41 weeks the American public has been privileged to a front row seat into all of the lives of these men. C-SPAN is a network that for the past 20 years has provided the ultimate in public affairs programming. The education department provides all of these programs and the teaching materials free to the schools in this country. It also gives the people a voice with the call-in show Washington Journal. C-SPAN is absolutely non-partisan. During the American President series I have learned so much. I have observed that many of them faced the same problems in office. Some of the recurrent issues are education, budget, taxes, health, and, unfortunately, race relations.

Tocqueville taught me that education, free press, and free speech are essential for a democracy to survive. In order to make this work, a country needs active citizens.

In my history class I felt the excitement and energy that the new settlers brought to this country. It was truly inspiring. Sometimes I think that all Americans are conceived with a special gene. It is the "First Amendment;" they all know it and woe to anyone who would try to take it away from them. For my friends in Europe, this is how the first amendment reads:

"Congress shall make no law respecting an establishment of religion, or prohibiting the free exercise thereof; or abridging the freedom of speech, or of the press, or the right of the people peacefully to assemble, and to petition the Government for a redress of grievances."

I was always proud to be a British subject and I was often asked how I could tolerate being "subjected." I never felt subjected except during the German Occupation of Jersey. I resented that and I never want to live under those circumstances again. The Americans do have some questions about a monarchy. To be honest, I see it with different eyes now. It would not work in this country. Often asked is why the Queen does not abdicate. I clearly remember her dedicating her life to the United Kingdom and I think at that time it was probably the Empire. I do not believe that abdication is a possibility for her. Queen Elizabeth meant that vow and she would keep her word. As monarch she is an integral part of the Constitution. It is a lifetime commitment.

As long as I am on the subject, and leaving personalities out of this discussion, I believe that the Prince of Wales job description represents the most dead end job ever to be written. How many of us would want to put our careers on hold until our parent died. It must be miserable. Does it take 50 years to learn to be a king? I do not know. None of this has anything to do with me now. I just offer it as a thought.

One of the things that I like about America is the lack of class-consciousness. I think such an attitude is artificial and often leads to shallow behavior. Truth is, and here is Tocqueville again, "money" is where it is at in this country. Even the most ordinary of us have the freedom to choose what we want to do if we can afford it. There remain too many inequities, in this country but given the chance and education, deep down there is opportunity.

Finally, I am interested in the politics of this country. I care that we must have a President of whom we can be proud. Elections mean that some are winners and others are losers, but there is always a tomorrow. I wonder, however, why the process has to take so long. I detest negative commercials. Why is it so impossible for any politician to simply state the issue and the plan to resolve it? Instead we first hear the individual's list of accomplishments and then how rotten the opponent is and maybe after all that we get a plan. I find it so frustrating. I can write all of my opinions because I have the right to express them freely (First Amendment). Something tells me that I have made my point. End of discussion.

CHAPTER TWENTY

The Girl By The Gun

This is the true account of a very special and unusual relationship in my life. It is a love story, not in a romantic sense, but of a deep affection that grew with the years. It is the story of a man and a young woman who met in the early summer of 1946. They were worlds apart in age, experience, wisdom, and maturity. It was a relationship that was to last for 34 years. Strange twists in our lives often turn out to be very important. What seemed to be an ordinary even insignificant meeting enriched my life.

One of the benefits at the London Hospital was that the student nurses had four weeks of vacation each year. I thought that was normal. It was an unpleasant shock to me when I found out later that this was luxury and that two weeks was all that I could expect in the real world. The month was divided into two two-week periods. May 1946 was my first time off during training and at long last I was able to go home. I had been placed on night duty probably in March of that year. We had been at the London for two or three months. It was the shock treatment, plain and simple. Immediately I discovered that I was unable to sleep during the daylight hours. I naturally did not anticipate this problem. Apart from being ill with hepatitis during the Occupation, I suppose I had never been up at night. It was a nightmare (pardon the expression) and a great disappointment. It was never the workload that bothered me. I felt exhausted the entire time. Sometimes I had only one or two hours sleep in 24 hours. I feared that I would have to leave the London and my friends.

The separation from the family had begun. I remember very little of those two weeks of vacation at home. I do remember the ride from the airport and walking into our home. It seemed to be so different and yet it was the same. I was different. I was happy to be in the Island again. It seemed like paradise to me after living in the East End of London. The Island was so clean and fresh. The sea was a sparkling blue; the white sandy beaches were shiny and clean washed by the tide, which was nearing the low tide mark. It all seemed to be so comfortable. One day during those two weeks Dad came home and told us that the Nuffield Organization was sending a representative over from the export division. This was a major automobile manufacturer located in Oxford, England, home of the University where so many of the Fulbright scholars from the United States have studied.

The Nuffield product was the full line of Morris cars. The "Morris Minor" was very suitable for the narrow roads and lanes in the Island. The Germans had seized most, if not all, of the cars during the Occupation and there was a need to get new ones back into the Island.

My father was the general manager of the Cleveland Garages and would be entertaining this man. My father was a wonderful guide; he knew every lane in the island. He loved to show off his beloved Jersey. He was a kind man who would do anything for anyone. I do not believe that he had an enemy during his entire life. My mother announced one day that we were taking this man out to dinner that night. His name was Robert Armstrong. Anne and I were included in the plans whether we wanted to go or not. I was eighteen and Anne must have been eleven years old. She essentially was a little girl.

Dad had arranged for the man to stay in a small hotel on the East Coast of the Island at La Rocque. This proved to be the ideal spot for Bob Armstrong. When the tide goes out as it does every twelve hours, it reveals a rocky beach. It is an interesting landscape and it is possible to walk out for a mile or more at low tide. Bob was a walker, not a stuffy official in a business suit. He was a warm and relaxed person. I was totally absorbed in my own problems, dreading the thought of returning to night duty, so I paid very little attention to the dinner conversation. As I look back, Bob was a special person, a "thoroughly decent chap," easy to be with and he certainly liked my parents. He appreciated Mother's cooking. The Jersey Royal potatoes were in season and for as long as I knew him he talked about those "tatties" as he called them. If I was bored, Anne must have felt more out of it than I did.

I vaguely remember three or more outings with this man but my memories are very vague. I do remember that he came to our home several times for meals during that two weeks in May. My vacation was soon over and my parents took me to the airport. If I had said one word of doubt about returning to the London, my father would have turned the car around and taken me home.

An elderly couple about my parent's age, were also passengers on the plane to London. I presume that they had been on vacation in the Island. My father was 48 and my mother was almost 46 but that was like the equivalent of 100-plus to me! The passengers I mentioned were John and Mary Simpson. They made a point of talking to me and insisted that I visit them at their home. I learned later that the basis for the invitation was they noticed how distraught my parents were at my departure. They were a great couple and I enjoyed their home very much. Their home was in Brentwood, Essex. The name of the house was Mount Rethy. The garden was typically English with a profusion of flowers of every color. Mary spent many hours tending it. Some months later I was assigned to the London Hospital Annex in Brentwood so I was able to ride my bike over to the house in my off duty. I have not thought of any of this for many years. It is strange that this memory comes back to me so easily. They were good people.

Soon after I returned from Jersey to the London I had my 19th birthday on June 1, 1946. I was surprised to receive a letter from Bob Armstrong in which he enclosed two pound notes. In the letter he told me that he admired the way I was sticking to the job and that he had no idea that I was less than 19 for he thought that when he met me I was about 23. Two pounds sterling was a windfall at the time. Pauline and I probably spent it on food. We were always hungry in those days and food was rationed.

We were very amused that a man about my parents' age sent me this letter. Actually he was 47 at the time, one year older than my mother. Age meant little to us; as far as we were concerned, there were "us" and the rest of the population of old people. My parents, both of whom looked younger than their years, were in the ancient classification. I wrote to thank Mr. Bob Armstrong for the gift and letter and never thought any more about it.

August 9 I received a long letter from him from Switzerland. He told me a story about climbing a mountain and the view that one sees at the top. He described a long walk he took climbing Mount Wellington in Tasmania (3,000 ft) in 1930. It was a hot day and he felt like a fool, but he got to the top. All the next week he was a hero for he had done what the natives had never tried and he found it so worthwhile. Bob became disillusioned with the Labor government in England. Disgusted is the more descriptive word. After agreeing to transfer to Switzerland and then to Rio de Janeiro in South America, his frustration extended toward the Nuffield Organization. Following what he considered political and commercial blunders, he quit the company. He considered the firm was making very poor business decisions, especially in South America where German products were so successful.

He moved to Western Australia where he found a new life. I described meeting Bob as a casual meeting. It was always with the family and the fact that I remember so little about it shows that it was not important to me at the time. I doubt that I met him more that half a dozen times. For the next 32 years he wrote to me, urging me on to the top of the next mountain that I needed to climb. I began to realize much later that life is a series of mountains and small victories. When he died, his housekeeper Mrs. Doris Everett wrote to me. She said that she did not feel that he was gone; his spirit would live on for he was a wonderful friend. He was cremated and his ashes were buried at his beloved property Riverdale. Earlier this year, Professor Sommerness suggested to me that I must check to see if Bob had any heirs. The reason for this advice was that I wanted to write about this special friend in my life. My search began. I tried the internet. I tried to find the name of the newspaper in that location. Finally, I wrote to the last address I had for Mrs. Everett. It was a senior residence. I wrote "Dear Administrator" and fate was on my side. Someone on the staff remembered Mrs. Everett's granddaughter, Julie. When I returned from Washington last June I found a letter from Mrs. Everett's daughter, Pat, waiting for me. Just a few moments ago I ran up to the mailbox and in it I found a second letter from Pat. Here am I writing about Bob. Sometimes life is stranger than fiction.

The Bob I remember, wherever his spirit rests, is chuckling with delight. Perhaps he is still looking out for me. I grew up in a time when children were to be seen and not heard. We knew that we were loved by implication and by actions. This love was, as far as I remember, never verbally expressed. Compliments were never given for fear that we might become conceited. This was not child abuse; it was the norm.

Bob Armstrong was the first person to treat me as an adult. He became a friend and a mentor who convinced me that I could become better than I could ever have imagined. It is important for me to remind myself that I had lived for five years, just as all the other Channel Islanders did, in a restricted environment, shut away from the normal world. I may have been 18 (and looked 23), but I was years younger in maturity.

I listened to my friends talk about their experiences as youngsters and I had missed so much. Bob's letters to me were honest, convincing and affectionate. I appreciate them now much more than I did as I was rushing to grow up. His message was beautifully written on any old piece of paper that he could find. I saved them for all of these years and through all of my many moves. This surprises me.

Bob loved his "Riverdale". He had established a new life, which brought him immense happiness. It was a move he never regretted. He followed his instinct and found his dream. He became a farmer. The land he purchased needed a lot of attention. It was hard physical work and he relished the challenge. He was his own boss.

He often wrote to me that work should be a hobby, not a dreary day-to-day existence.

He meant a lot to me over the 30-plus years of correspondence. When I received the news of his death in 1980, I knew that I had lost someone whom I cared for deeply and who was a very special friend. I cried more for him than I had done for my father. I knew Bob for longer in a different way and, besides, I was an American now and my emotions were not smothered by reserve.

If he were alive today this is the letter that I would write to him:

Dear Bob,

Your last letter to me is dated February 2, 1980, so we have a lot of catching up to do. I am happily retired since 1992. You were in on the beginning, but you were not here to see the end. In 1993, I moved to another area in Mesa in what is known as a "planned community." The houses are what you would call semi-detached. There are only 122 units and they are tucked in neatly away from the main road. The development is called Camino Del Rey, which I believe is the King's Road. It is perfect for me. When I decided to make the move, my house sold in three hours for cash. I walked the floor all night (it was a Friday) wondering where in the world I was going to go with two dogs. By the Sunday morning, I was the new owner of this house. Anne's twins, Tricia and Michele, thought I had lost it. They hurried out to see the new house (subtly telling me that it was close to an extended care facility should I need it). Tuffy, Chip, and I moved in five weeks later. Tuffy and Chip were my last dogs. Darcy, my cat whose picture you admired died some years before.

Before I retired I became a hospice nurse working in the community. Part of my area of responsibility was in the Superstition Mountains. They are beautiful and forbidding. Legend has it than an old Dutchman had buried treasure somewhere out there and to date no one has ever found the treasure.

I enjoyed the work, but I must admit that I always hoped that I would not be called out into the mountains at night. It was pitch black out there and I would have been scared stiff.

Yesterday, I read all of your 34 letters once more. They are as relevant today as they were when you wrote them, except that now I understand your advice so much more. Why does it take a person so long to realize this? I asked myself that question many times. Your words are a gift from you. Your friendship and affection shine through your words. They warm my heart (ageing heart, what a terrible thought). I hope that it beats on for a good while longer because I am having fun with this retirement thing.

A few thoughts on some of the wisdom you shared with me over the years. You wrote over and over again about the photo you took of me by a German gun on one of the outings with the family. I never saw the photo. You so often refer to me as the "girl by the gun," When you died Mrs. Everett and her daughter searched for it among your papers. You always told me that you kept my photos in the herd book, but "the girl by the gun" was never found.

This is some of what you wrote:

"Don't you remember going out with Dad and Anne to a small tea room along the coast one afternoon, when a photo was taken of you by a German gun on the left bank from Anne? It is in my mind now. And you looked nice but lonely standing in the road. The bank on your right sloped toward the sea."

Here are some other things that you wrote:

"Hello, Little One!   October 1, 1948
A nice letter, and it pleases me no end that you enjoy that scramble up the rocky mountain. You will remember the view that I have always promised you at the top? I think that you have immense courage and it has been more than interesting to watch you grow, for you are different from the days of Jersey, some eighteen months ago. You presented a very pleasing contrast to your sister Anne, and it was not easy to think that you were sisters, Anne being so appealing in a different way.

to think that you were sisters, Anne being so appealing in a different way.

Anne I think will reach great heights marrying some local lad and being maternal and very contented. You, at the first time of meeting were "mousey" and apart, and you had little to say, although like Tim's parrot you did not have much to say, because you thought a lot. You will be more easily hurt than Anne, but you will rise further than ever she could and the training has brought out from your quiet interior a strength which can never be taken from you. Home will be just the same value to you, but the small things that meant all to you in the Island are not of the same worth now, for your extension of brain has taken you worlds away from them. Yours is the feeling that comes to anyone away from home, and life without it would be without its salt."

"Mousey" (The computer does not like that word perhaps it will accept "mouse like") It means nondescript. Yes, I have a computer, isn't that amazing? I never wanted one but never is a dangerous word that one should not use unless one wants whatever it is to happen.

Bob, at the time I first met you I was wrapped in misery at the prospect of going back to night duty. At that age, three more years of training felt like a life sentence. How I wish three years today would last as long as those seemed to be at the time.

Your wisdom is too valuable to be left in my desk drawer. You were really frank.

After the girl by the gun episode you wrote:

"I think that you will have a lonelier time for a start for you think rare for a woman, and existence amid crowds does not seem to have any great appeal. You expect more than the complacent and you will achieve more but I think that you will do it on your own. Perhaps we are a little bit the same?"

On reflection I do not think that I have been lonely, certainly not now. I feel much happier in a small group because I like people and that pleasure is lost for me in a crowd. I am content doing things on my own, but I like to do things that are comfortable. I am not the type to rough it. I was very shy and lacking in self-knowledge when I met you. Your letters over the years gave me encouragement.

It was a slow process but you were always there urging on to the glorious view that I would find at the top of the mountain.

Bob, when my father died you understood how that would change our lives and you were so encouraging about my mother's decision to come to America. Anne was unhappy about leaving Jersey as you predicted but Mother said "we" are going and that was it. Anne was 18 at the time.

You wrote when I decided to visit America in 1952:

"You will like the American brightness and efficiency: Sheila I know that your choice is a good one, one that will range from the Hudson to the Yosemite Valley. See things but never be amazed at anything those disciples of publicity may say or do."

(Bob should see the newspaper ads and the television commercials today.)

In 1950 you wrote:

"Many congratulations on getting the final. Grand work in which I always aimed to have a hand. From your first letters I felt that the East End was wearing holes into your soul and so each time I wrote I tried to do something to cheer you on. I wonder if you ever sensed my wish to make you succeed? I always pictured you as you were when I took the photo of the German gun on that bank half way down the hill. You were away from the family and you seemed to be suddenly alone. I got the impression then that you would go far but that it might be a very lonely roe to hoe and that impression was with me when you wrote of the foulness of the London slums. Anne is so different, very easy going and far less complicated then her sister. In your next letter you can explain to me what grade of BF (bloody fool) I am, but all the same I am delighted that you have got through for you have something they can never take away and you will stand out from the herd with their full time hobbies of darts and ale."

Bob, in scanning the letters you wrote to me over the years you consistently refer to me as the "girl by the gun." You explained often that in spite of all the photos that I sent you of my mother, Anne, and the five nippers, as you called them, (Anne's children) your thoughts always went back to me by that German gun. That moment for you was fixed in time. I find that to be incredibly amazing. I struggle to remember that moment. Sometimes I sense that I walked away to be alone but as the memory comes into my mind it darts away once more. Neither of us could ever have imagined that it would never fade for all of our lifetimes. That moment, so ordinary, so fleeting, formed our relationship forever. You came as part of the package along with each mountain. You helped me to the top of each one.

I went back and looked at your description of your farm. You never sent the promised photo because you said that your camera was left in a cab in Berlin just before WW11. You were in Munich at the time, just three days before the war began. Did it never occur to you to buy a new one? There are disposable cameras now. So many products are disposable, except all of the things in life that really count.

This is what you wrote about your farm:

"I have had the immense luck to get a twin block property of 230 acres with an orchard and a mile of river frontage along the Kalgan

The trees are mostly hardwoods and what with new growth and an aged monarch falling in past bush fires there is a lot to be done. Good sport in shorts and shirt. I was wise in my decision to work for myself; if one likes work of the hard type one can get things done and not have to wait in vain for decisions from above that never come."

Some years later you wrote:

"By the time we make this dam for irrigation, haymaking will be with us and so the years slide away. Farming is most fascinating and I know of no better way of losing one's life savings."

In 1967 you wrote:

"The small farm provides a nice living together with some savings, which the inevitable inflation is making weaker and weaker each year."

You enlarged the farm, bulldozing and clearing until you had 100 more acres for grass. As you were writing you shot a hawk that was raiding a fowl run. Later you added cattle, but they must not have been Jerseys' for you surely would have told me about that. I was surprised when you sold the farm in 1973 that it was so easy for you. I suppose those of us, and I am one of them, who can walk away from our life's work happily are among the most lucky ones in this world.

Bob, you always feared for the vulnerability of Australia. You wrote of Russian ships in the Indian Ocean and of the fear of China descending one day onto Australia. While the Australians are able to provide even a token force to help the Americans, you (the Australians) think that they will never forget you.

Bob, just recently Australian troops were sent to end a cruel and vicious civil war in East Timor, as part of the United Nations peacekeeping force. China continues to rattle the West and the Great Russian bear that you described is temporarily lame. Germany is one country. The Americans have taken over first place and are often called to fill the former British role of policing the world. A fact you had predicted. You disliked the Labor government. Labor is in power in Britain. I have yet to hear any of my friends rejoice about it. You talked a lot about automobile engines and how long you were able to keep your Datsun on the road. You were always interested in what I was driving. Well I have a Honda Civic hatchback and I would like it to last forever!

When I became an American citizen you wrote:

"You were very wise to become an American for it is a citizenship to be envied."

warm and hospitable people, often misunderstood by the rest of the world. My sincere hope is that when I am in this country I can be the best Channel Islander and when I go to Jersey I can be the best American. I am proud to be a Channel Islander but I would never renounce my United States citizenship.

I have all of your letters. I flinched when I read that so often you asked me for a reply. You cannot read this but if I were able I would give you my love and so many thanks for the push you always gave me towards the top of the mountain. For your faith that I could always accomplish more than I believed to be possible. February 2 1980 you started your last letter to me, "Darling Girl by the Gun (one of our first walks in Jersey.)"

August 2, 1980, you died in your sleep.

Everyone should have a friend like you. Rest well in Heaven for you surely must be there.

Your devoted "Girl by the Gun."
Sheila.

CHAPTER TWENTY-ONE

Friendship

When I was born, Dr. Mortimer Evans noticed a mole on my back. He said, "Mole on the back, money by the sack." The money never quite materialized but I have been rich in other ways. Given a choice of one or the other, I would choose friends all the time. Money can be spent, lost in the market, and too often attract the wrong friends. Friendship pays dividends for a lifetime.

At the beginning of this adventure I asked a few friends to write me a letter of anecdotes and memories through the years. I chose friends from my student days (fellow sufferers) and one or two others. To all of the rest of my friends, I ask that they accept my thoughts as if they were directed to them and them alone.

Pam Carver (Millard) was my first school friend at Mandalay School. We had some happy times together. Both of us were shy (what a pair). Pam's parents had a small grocery store. Its name will live forever; the corner where it was located is officially known as " Millards Corner." Pam's family was from Somerset, England. It was Pam who had a starring role with me at school by refusing to recite "Daffodils."

Pam remembers that we enjoyed putting on concerts and that we had to bribe the two Annes to take part. Pam's sister Anne was the same age as my sister Anne. Pam and her sister Anne were part of the fivesome during the air raid. Later they were deported to Germany. I was devastated when my friend left. We are in touch now and Pam describes herself as my "oldest friend."

I have friends that were an "only" child and Pauline was one of them. I have written often in this book about how good her family was to me during our student days at the London. The amazing thing is that we can pick up the phone and talk together as if it were yesterday. We share that common bond of being student nurses at the

London. Pauline could never wait for the next train, we always had to run for the one that was just leaving the station. Pauline, I wonder if you can still do that?

Ida was my friend from the frozen north. Yes, Ida, it was cold outside, but nothing can equal that green bathtub in the upstairs section of the house. I dare to say that if the tap were still dripping the tub would not be full yet. Far better to be the maid and use the bath in the downstairs section of the house.

In 1959 I met another only child, Betty Brennan. We met in Bermuda. Betty had a steady boyfriend, Ray. Ray was an engineer in the Merchant Marine and he was overseas at the time. Betty had just received her Master's degree in nursing from Boston College. Her mother was horrified that she went on vacation and thought that she should get a job and start earning some money. Betty had other ideas. I first met Ray when he took us in a very tiny, rowboat around Salem harbor in Massachusetts. I was at their wedding and our friendship is deep and abiding. They have taught me to love New England. Their home is mine and I never had a bad day in their company. Salem and Marblehead are rich in Channel Island history. That dates back to the days when Salem was a busy New England seaport.

The following excerpts are from letters I have received from my dear friends:

From Pauline:

Sheila and I started our training at London Hospital to become nurses in October 1945 at the tender age of 18+. I really cannot remember the first occasion on which we met, but soon, out of all of the other girls in the group, I began to recognize someone whose company I could enjoy. Sheila was a lively but rather nervous person, afraid of doing the wrong thing, due largely to her lack of confidence. She was also not very big, and for some peculiar reason I nicknamed her Winkle, or Wink, which in fact stuck until about 20 years ago (I bet she hated the name.)

229

From Ida:

It is a privilege to call Sheila Le Sueur my friend! Our friendship has spanned almost 50 years. We met when we were 22 years old. We were pupil midwives at St. Helier Hospital in Carshalton in Surrey England.

There were 20 nurses on our course, all qualified in general nursing. The majority arrived in Carshalton with a friend. Four of us were alone. Lorna Davis came from St. Bartholomew's Hospital, Maureen Connoly from Belfast Royal Infirmary, NI., Sheila from the London Hospital in Whitechapel. I came from the Bradford Royal Infirmary in Bradford in Yorkshire. We four have kept in touch ever since. Our time together at St. Helier was not all work. The premature babies were a particular joy to Sheila.

No one could pronounce her surname. Richard Dimbleby, the well-known broadcaster in England, wrote a book and he used the surname Le Sueur for one of the characters in his book. This individual was given the nickname of "Drains." (The English people pronounced Le Sueur as "Le Sewer." Sheila got the name amongst our group. She shared in the fun, but wrote to Richard Dimbleby to inform him of the correct pronunciation, which is "Le Swer" – and he wrote back!

Readers please note: "the name thing continues." I no longer have a nickname, probably because no one spells Sheila or Le Sueur correctly!

From Newell Younggren:

Dear Sheila,

This is a thank you note with memories – some good, some bad.

During the early 1920s, at age of five, I knew there was a Jersey – not New Jersey, but an island. Where, I had not the faintest. Pacific? Atlantic? Indian? My father had a herd of Jersey cows – the best! And they originated from this island.

Ultimately, through a strange experience, I found the island! Many years later, during the war, I was sleeping in a real bed with clean sheets - the first bed, sheets, and pajamas in over six months -

in a lovely seaside hotel in Granville, France. We were 500 miles behind the front lines, but the Germans raided and four of us were taken by life raft, small boat, and tug to St. Helier, Jersey, where we were imprisoned, along with several dozen other allied soldiers and seamen. The episode started 1 March 1945 and ended 9 May 1945. The "episode" was sad, thrilling, challenging, and revealing. Here, on a 45 square mile island were thousands of German troops, 30,000 or more civilians, and our little stalag. Here, we later learned, were occupied and occupiers struggling against all odds for survival. No food, very little energy, no medicine, human beings with diverse points of view, all locked together, ultimately to see the conflict of these interests terminate in a positive, constructive conclusion.

During the next 50+ years scores of people have reviewed the history of this occupation, gaining respect for the determination of great people of all genders, creeds, philosophies, and moral values. The occupation by the Germans was a classic in Military Government as the civilian population reflected controlled tolerance while resisting the indignity of enemy military presence and strange values.

The efforts of the Occupation Society involving hundreds of people brought to mind my first contacts with Margaret and Michael Ginns and resulted in knowing many other Jerseites. The island and its occupation struggle became real. For example, we saw the interesting interpretation of that Baron Hans Max von Aufsess and the Channel Islands Occupation Review edited by Peter Bryans, the Granville Raid by Michael Ginns, and the heroic episodes relating to Dr. John Lewis. These, along with many other viewpoints, made the Channel Islands, particularly Jersey, an important part of our lives.

We American G.I.s have made Jersey our adopted home in large part because of the efforts of Sheila Le Sueur and her sister, Anne, who, in 1995, brought a number of us together for the 50th anniversary of the liberation of 9 May 1945.

Newell Younggren

P.S. I have many memories of the POW days, but that which stands out was the fact that the Jerseites sent a fresh egg to each of us for Easter 1945 while the population was literally starving. Honestly!

From Richard Royer, M.D.:

In Michigan, during World War II, the Sisters of Bon Secours converted their Grosse Pointe, Michigan, nursing home into a 33 bed community hospital. At the same time, on the Isle of Jersey, a young Sheila Le Sueur, her parents and sister were under Nazi subjugation. During the next 10 years, both Sheila and Bon Secours progressed in an admirable fashion and came together the 19th of May, 1955.

By then Sheila had completed her nursing training in London and had considered numerous far flung places about the globe to apply her skills. Her family urged her first to visit relatives in the United States before lighting out on her own to places where she knew no one. Sheila arrived on Thanksgiving 1952. She readily found work, but she soon left several institutions that hadn't measured up to her standards.

However, after visiting a patient at the then expanded 160 bed Bon Secours Hospital, Sheila was favorably impressed. She accepted the $13.50/day position to work in the old wing of that growing hospital. It didn't take long for the good Sisters to realize what a gem they had. This bundle of focused energy was given increasingly greater responsibility. Members of the Medical Staff trusted her with techniques typically reserved for singularly trained individuals, confident that her actions would be appropriate and well within her realm of competence.

When Bon Secours started its Intensive Care Unit, many of the old guard surgeons complained that premium surgical beds had been usurped. Their angst increased when Sheila, who had studied the feasibility of establishing a certifiable Coronary Care Unit, got the okay and opened the ward Thanksgiving Day 1967. More surgical beds were lost for a while, but the bustling, persevering Sheila and her hand-picked nurses developed a state-of-the-art unit that was enviable. No longer was Bon Secours an inconsequential enterprise when she retired in 1977. It had grown both in size and respectability. Her contributions to the institution were considerable.

Throughout her stay at Bon Secours Sheila remained gossip-free, incorruptible, unaffected and unassuming as she performed the full spectrum of nursing activities... starched and impeccably attired as the day she arrived.

R.R.Royer, M.D.

From Joan Kettel:

Dear Sheila,

I first knew you in the early '60s when you were a charge nurse and I was a candy striper and, later, an aide. You were very efficient and professional, and I was in awe of you.

Then again in '65 I knew you as an administrator. You hired me as a new grad, and you were very kind and welcoming. Then as a co-worker in ICU. You were very easy to work with and I had been very worried about facing you as an equal, having known you as an administrator. I admired the way you worked with the patients. You were exactly as you are; nothing was hidden.

Then I knew you as my head nurse in CCU. You were encouraging, helpful, caring and always inspiring us to do better. It was wonderful.

Then we were both head nurses, me in ICU and you in CCU. This was the flowering of our friendship. It was paradise. We had so much fun, I often said we shouldn't be paid. And you taught me so much about myself, both as a person and as a nurse. I remember you helping me write the minutes for my first ICU meeting, and you encouraged me (prodded, really) into teaching for Michigan Heart. Never would I have done it without you. Now from here on I know you as my best friend, always there for me, always truthful and honest, always ready to listen and share both the good times and the bad, and always accepting of me just the way I am.

Sometimes we are really lucky. A wonderful person enters our life and becomes an integral part of it. That is the way I feel about you and our friendship. For that I will always be grateful.

Love Joan.

CHAPTER TWENTY-TWO

Another Door Opens

This afternoon I was looking for a document in an old metal filing box, as I need to make arrangements for some repair work on our family grave in Jersey, Channel Islands. I came across a plain envelope and I looked inside. I was astonished to find two holy cards from funerals. They were from the funerals of Mr. R. Robert Geniusz and Mr. John R. Gariepy. These are the names of the patients of whom I wrote of in my chapter on ICU. I can only presume that I brought the cards among other papers when I moved from Michigan. Mr. Geniusz was the electrical engineer with intractable ventricular tachycardia. Mr. Gariepy was the man successfully defibrillated after the decision was made that efforts to revive him had failed. I was alone at home and I am awed by my discovery.

I immediately called Joan (Yuhase) Kettel in Michigan. Both of us remember these good men as if it were yesterday. It occurred to me that these individuals are heroes. They were patients at a time when there was little that could be done to help them, apart from comfort measures and traditional therapy. They were pioneers in a very real sense. Millions have reason to be grateful to them. We were privileged to care for them.

Joan and I both recognize the fact that dear Mr. Geniusz, as an electrical engineer, knew more about the equipment than either of us did at that time. In fact, he often helped us figure out the monster of a machine. He would say, "green is the ground" when we hooked him up to the monitor.

Modern day nurses and perhaps physicians may find this basic care very crude. Lidocaine had not made its appearance. None of the modern medications of today were on the horizon. It is worth considering the lightening strides made in cardiology in recent years.

We must all be grateful for the progress that we so often take for granted. I cannot stress strongly enough how exciting it was to be a nurse in those days. We began to believe and to see that a heart attack did not have to lead to death. We had the joyful experience of seeing many of our patient's return to their families. It was an exhilarating feeling and I can still feel the excitement of coming on duty each day.

I consider that Mr. Geniusz and Mr. Gariepy set me on a path in my career that I should cherish forever. I have the feeling that once more they are with me helping me to tell their story. I hope that they can feel my caring and gratitude.

Throughout my career, I never ever violated patient confidentiality. Finding these cards was so dramatic for me, it seemed as if the men were speaking to me. This is how I choose to honor them, their contribution, and their memory.

CHAPTER TWENTY-THREE

Reflections

A few moments ago I realized that I am completing this part of my journey at the end of the Century! This is a deep and overwhelming thought. I believe that this is only a pause; it is the fact that I am on this journey at all that is so amazing to me. I find it to be so exciting! I have done something that would never have occurred to me - write a book! I would never have believed it was within my capabilities. It is now beginning to look like a book!

At this point, I have absolutely no idea how it will be received, or even if it will be in print. I wonder what it would be like to see it, hold it in my hand. Will others read it? Will they pull it apart? Will I suffer if that happens? If it is successful, will this feeling of total disbelief disappear? What if it is a success? How will I handle it? What if it is a miserable failure, will I endure? That, at least, I know I can do. Will I be disappointed if it bombs? Of course! I did not set out to fail. I know that I can survive; I have had some experience with that. I sense that this is just a pause in my journey; its not the end.

Apart from putting my memories on paper, have I accomplished something that will encourage others to find their way to their own adventures? I hope so.

What is around the next corner? That is an impossible question to answer. But I do know that this fall, Anne and I will be in Jersey for one month. My nieces Sheila, Tricia, Michele and her husband John, will join us for a week, as will other dear friends. So much to see and to do, and so many friends to visit. I want to visit the village of Tocqueville in Normandy. Alexis de Tocqueville and his writings on democracy were the impetus for so much that has happened to me for the last two years. I hope that I am able to visit the Chateau, see his desk where he wrote Democracy in America. That is a very good thought to start the Century.

There are for all of us personal questions that come to mind. Different lives, experiences, choice of work and lots of evaluating to do. I always felt deep down that nursing was my choice. It was good for me. Not lucrative, but survivable. (There are not many student nurses who can be described as affluent.) The London was the right place for me even though I hated some of it. I am proud of my accomplishments in that part of my life. Bob Armstrong always told me that work should be a hobby. I agree.

Friends also have been of paramount importance to me. The formula is simple: find and make the right friendships. That is a real joy in life. My friends are my sustenance.

What have I learned that I can share with others? Perhaps that shyness, so overwhelming, can be overcome. Once that is accomplished, it is banished forever. Maturity helps, but it is more than that. Shyness wastes opportunity and it is torture to be paralysed by it. Release from this handicap allows us to see and appreciate others more. But some are not appealing, so just let them be. It simply means allowing oneself to be real and enjoy each encounter. It works like magic.

I seem to be giving advice that I am not professionally qualified to do. These thoughts are simply of my experiences. I feel that I can meet anyone anywhere any time. That is a refreshing and stimulating feeling. It is freedom.

Learning in retirement dispels the myth that we lose it when we become "elderly." I detest that word. I want to go on learning as long as I am able. It is such fun and the possibilities are endless. There is so much in this world. Education is an adventure, especially when there are no examinations. It is easy to imagine how dull my life would be without the opportunities that each day brings. Freedom to choose is such a privilege. Always remembers that.

Last night I tried to tell Dr. Royer how much I appreciated him and his guidance with this book. He said, "Pass it on." I pass it on.

Sheila holding alabaster bust of Alexis de Tocqueville, March 2000.

REFERENCES

1. The German Occupation of the Channel Islands. The Official History of the Occupation Years. Charles Cruickshank.
2. The Channel Islands Occupation and Liberation. Asa Briggs.
3. The German Occupation of Jersey. L.P, Sinel.
4. A Doctor's Occupation. Dr. John Lewis.
5. Lest We Forget. Roy Thomas.
6. Balleine's History of Jersey. Marguerite Syvret and Joan Stevens.
7. The Von Aufsess Occupation Diary. Baron Von Aufsess.
8. The Memoirs of Lord Coutanche - A Jerseyman looks back. Compiled by H.R.S. Pocock.
9. The London. A.E. Clark- Kennedy.
10. World Book and Encyclopedia.
11. Living the Values: The Sisters of Bon Secours in Michigan.
12. A Century of Caring.The Sisters of Bon Secours in the United States. 1881-1981 Sister Mary Cecilia O' Sullivan , C.B.S.
13. Tocqueville in America. George Wilson Pierson.
14. Democracy in America. Alexis de Tocqueville.
15. The Encyclopedia of American Facts and Dates. Gorton Carruth.
16. The Federalist. Alexander Hamilton - James Madison - John Jay. Edited by Benjamin F. Wright.
17. America and Its Peoples. Martin- Roberts-McMurry-Jones.
18. C-SPAN. Exploring Democracy in America.
19. The Constitution of The United States. National Constitution Center.
20. The Royal London Hospital. A Brief History. Sheila M Collins.
21. Mission 2000 Praying Scripture in a Contemporary Way. Mark Link, S.J.

OTHER PUBLICATIONS FROM

STARLIGHT PUBLISHING

SEE DETAILS OF THESE AND MANY OTHER CHANNEL ISLAND
PUBLICATIONS ON OUR WEBSITE www.aacbooks.co.uk

STARLIGHT
IMPORTS DISTRIBUTION PUBLISHING

UNIT 3B, BARETTE COMMERCIAL CENTRE
LA ROUTE DU MONT MADO
ST.JOHN, JERSEY, CHANNEL ISLANDS, JE3 4DS
TEL. 44 (0)1534 860806   FAX. 44 (0)1534 860811
E-MAIL sales@aacbooks.co.uk